D0097871

18838

WHITE RABBIT

WHITE RABBIT

A Doctor's Story of Her Addiction and Recovery

Martha A. Morrison, M.D.

Crown Publishers, Inc.
New York

Grateful acknowledgment is hereby given to Almo Publications for permission to reprint lyrics from "White Rabbit," words and music by Grace Slick, copyright © 1967 by Irving Music, Inc. (BMI). All rights reserved. International copyright secured.

Published by Crown Publishers, Inc., 225 Park Avenue South, New York, New York 10003

CROWN is a trademark of Crown Publishers, Inc.

Manufactured in the United States of America

Library of Congress Cataloging-in-Publication Data
Morrison, Martha A.,
White Rabbit: a doctor's story of her addiction and recovery/Martha A. Morrison.
p. cm.
1. Morrison, Martha A., Drug use. 2. Women physicians—Drug use. 3. Women physicians—United States—Biography.
I. Title.
RC564.5.W66M67 1988
616.86′3′00924—dc 19
[B]   88-14964
ISBN 0-517-56816-0

10 9 8 7 6 5 4 3 2 1

First Edition

In memory of Mammy and Aunt Tude

and

*To all who have suffered
because of the disease of addiction.
May you be blessed with hope and recovery.*

CONTENTS

PREFACE   ix

1   *Visions of Paradise*   1

2   *Daddy's Little Girl*   9

3   *The Acid Smile*   19

4   *Born to Shoot Speed*   33

5   *No Easy Way Out*   46

6   *My World in a Syringe*   60

7   *The Needle and the Damage Done*   78

8   *The Making of a Junkie Doctor*   90

9   *Dr. Addict*   106

10   *Apocalypse Now*   124

11   *The Miracle Begins*   144

12   *Midnight Sunrise*   172

13   *Journey Without a Destination*   187

14   *Blood, Sweat, and Golden Opportunities*   207

15   *Florida Fantasies*   222

16   *One Day at a Time*   232

PREFACE

What follows is the story of an addict: a little girl who from the age of twelve stole her mother's painkillers; a rebellious teenager who smoked, drank, ate, and shot up virtually every drug imaginable; a young woman—a young woman doctor—who surreptitiously bombarded her body with so many drugs, from alcohol to heroin, that she almost died. Like all tales of addiction, this is a rather flamboyant story replete with violence, crime, treachery, deceit, out-of-control sexual escapades, suicide attempts, and profound human suffering.

It's my story—the story of my life, my loves, my near-deaths, my craziness, and the insanity of my addiction. For seventeen years, I lost myself in a wilderness of pain. But unlike many such stories, I'm happy to say, my tale has a joyous ending. Yes, I came—kicking and screaming, despite my desperate pain—to seek and ultimately to find a certain truth of my own—a special happiness, and true peace and serenity.

In this book, I have made every effort to be as candid as possible. I have changed many names and altered a few details to protect the privacy of others. Pseudonyms have also been used to protect the anonymity of those involved in twelve-step self-help groups. With these exceptions, the changes are minimal; and all of the statements about myself are my perceptions of the truth.

I tell my story in the hope that those who read it—especially those who suffer from addiction, whether they are addicts themselves or loved ones of addicts—will realize that recovery is possible. There is hope for a life free of drugs; there is hope for a life of peace, serenity, and productivity.

I must add that I speak only for myself; I am not telling this story on behalf of any other person or organization. I am, however, donating all proceeds from this book to three organizations dedicated to aiding those who suffer from addiction.

The writing and publication of this book would not have been possible without the help of a number of people:

First and foremost, I thank my parents for their unshakable confidence in me, their support, and their love. They lived through a long, shattering experience with me and, in a million ways, always stood by me—no matter what. I love them dearly.

I also thank my brother for being the best brother in the whole world, and I am grateful to him for his unwavering support and love.

I would like to thank my father-in-law, Dr. Doug Talbott, for two extremely important items: saving my life and introducing me to my husband. Since the moment I met him, Doug Talbott has always been there for me and with me. His interpretations of the "disease" and "recovery" were the only ones that made sense to me. Without him, I would have died.

I feel blessed that Doug and Polly Talbott introduced me to their rather special son, Doug Talbott, Jr. With "Fog" I have found a unique relationship, and with him, I share a special life and love.

I also thank all those people who are mentioned in the book. I believe each individual at every stage of my life played an extremely important part. I'm especially thankful to those who graciously gave of their time for interviews for this book. These people helped me to piece together the puzzle of my life and, at last, to begin to see it as a complete and meaningful whole.

Most particularly, I'd like to thank Dr. Art Moore, Suzanne Jones Schwartz, Brad Williams, Cyndy Knoke, Mark Knoke, Jill Knoke, Dr. Charles Greene, Jim O'Quin, Dr. Gregg Krulin, Dr. Emile Eckart, Mary Paal, Dr. Nick Paal, Dr. Henry Irby, Dr. Rick Bell, Dr. Jim Alley, Dr. Art Carpenter, Donnie Brown, Polly Talbott, all second- and third-generations Talbotts, Tray Morrison, John Morrison, J. R. Suter, Blanche Woodward, Dr. Harold Smith, and Dr. Philip Wilson.

A special thank-you must go to Sue Otts, who has been my secretary for five years. Her tireless efforts arranging speaking appointments, scheduling trips, dealing with patients, and helping me formulate new programs has been of immeasurable help to me. I could not have survived without her.

At Crown Publishers, I owe thanks to Barbara Grossman, Kate Hammon, Erica Marcus, and Pamela Thomas. I owe particular special thanks to Pam, who has guided and assisted me throughout the writing and publishing process. Without her, my story simply could not have been told in this way. Her contributions to this book and to my personal life have been immeasurable, and she has become throughout this journey a very special friend to me.

I want to thank Georgia Alcohol and Drug Associates and Ridgeview Institute for making a host of outstanding professional opportunities available to me. My partners and friends at GADA have been particularly supportive and caring.

Most important, I want to thank Alcoholics Anonymous and Narcotics Anonymous for the self-help programs they provide. I believe God's grace has been made manifest in the miracle of my life, and I am deeply grateful for the gift of recovery and the ability and opportunity to carry this message of love and hope.

WHITE RABBIT

One pill makes you larger
And one pill makes you small,
And the ones that Mother gives you
        don't do anything at all.
Go ask Alice...
When she's ten feet tall!

And if you go chasing rabbits,
And you know you're going to fall,
Tell them a hookah-smoking caterpillar
        has given you the call.
Call Alice...
When she was just small!

When men on chessboards
        get up and tell you where to go,
And you've just had some kind of mushroom
        and your mind is moving along,
Go ask Alice; I think she'll know!

When logic and proportion have fallen,
        I'll be dead,
And the white knight is talking backwards
And the red queen is on her head...

Remember what the dormouse said:
Feed your head!
Feed your head!!

GRACE SLICK
The Jefferson Airplane, 1967

1
VISIONS OF PARADISE

life is a bummer
it's a downer all the way
what a way to go
it's the long road to hell.

who knows where to turn
which way to go?
confusion, disillusion
surrounds us all.
                    MARTHA MORRISON, 1969

*September 12, 1979. 2:15 P.M. I have just injected 75
milligrams of pure methamphetamine hydrochloride—speed—intravenously. This is one of the most
startling revelations of my lifetime. The reason I'm
writing now is that this is probably the second-to-
last time I will take this drug. For me, this situation
is different.*

*I have used speed intermittently for a decade. I
have been addicted psychologically in the past on
several occasions. I have had my entire life fall
apart as a result of this mysterious drug.*

*Nine years ago I was under the care of a psychia-
trist for eighteen months and was hospitalized in a
psychiatric institution for three months. At that time
I lost everything I had because of speed—friends,
family, school, job, my mind, and my dignity. I have*

since recovered, finished school, and earned my M.D. degree. I am a medical doctor, a practicing psychiatrist—and a good one.

As I said, this is probably the next-to-last time I will ever inject amphetamines. I have just one comparable dose left. It is important that my feelings are recorded because I think I must be the world's expert on amphetamine abuse. I've studied its pharmacology, and I've worked with many drug-abuse patients. For ten years I have, in every way, abused this drug, although I have used it solely for task-oriented purposes.

There is nothing—I repeat, nothing—in the world comparable to a "speed rush." The instantaneous bombardment of all the senses as soon as these substances are injected intravenously, the sudden force of feeling, and always the element of the unexpected perpetuates the desire for this experience. Multivaried sensations involve all five of the senses—hearing, taste, smell, sight, and touch.

To most people who use speed, the taste of hydrochloride, which is intense immediately after injection, is unpleasant, if not offensive. To me, the taste is pleasing, since it is associated with other good feelings.

A roar like the ocean's surf grows and fills my head. The antiseptically sweet hydrochloride taste tingles in my mouth. My vision becomes slightly blurred. I can look intensely inside myself for a few minutes and enjoy the experience of knowing and feeling all these marvelous physical and emotional sensations. My heart rate and respiration increase dramatically. The top of my head feels as if it is leaving my body and going into orbit; I am unable to move or to attend to any outside stimuli immediately after the injection.

I concentrate on feeling, really feeling, all the sensations and perceptions; I am acutely aware. In some instances, I experience sexual sensations— sometimes an orgasm. My body tingles, my mind begins to race. Pleasurable electriclike shocks run through my entire body. I feel slightly disoriented for the first few minutes, in awe at the incredible power of this chemical substance.

It's unbelievable. Fascinating. Pleasurable. It is the need for intense stimulation from whatever source that drives individuals like me to seek this type of experience. We are people who need and demand an overwhelming amount of stimulation. We are not moderates. Routine everyday occurrences do not supply enough stimulation for us and therefore do not generally meet our needs. In a way, we are in a constant state of deprivation if we are unable to arrange for more intense stimulation. This constant deprivation leads to repeated abuse of amphetamines and amphetaminelike substances.

People like us are unique. We need to be productive, and we must be placed in situations where we can excel as a consequence of the same personality characteristics that lead us to drug use initially. We have enormous amounts of energy, even without artificial stimulants. We must substitute other behavior for drug use—while we are totally involved with the drug, but before prolonged use has occurred. This is imperative, as prolonged use of intravenous amphetamines can and does lead to serious, even fatal, medical and psychological consequences.

I would not trade my experiences with speed—good or bad—for anything. I have used and abused this drug, and it has done the same with me. I have grown and learned from my drug-related experiences. I am a better person because of them. I probably will never do speed again after I use this one remaining dose. I have substituted a great deal in its place, and I have consequently been rewarded and fulfilled. It took me ten years to develop this insight, ten years to feel that I am able to control my desire for this drug and not let it control me. I am successful and happy in every sense. I could have been dead, degenerate, worthless, if certain things had been different. But they weren't and I'm here to tell this story.

4:00 P.M. I did it. The grand finale! Must have been close to 100 milligrams total. Blew my head off! The taste in the back of my throat. The surf pounding and pounding. Immense body rushes. Vision blurred. Arrhythmias. Tachycardia. Ah, but the power. The wonderful, intense feeling of the rush. Magnificent! May be the best of all in ten years. Fantastic! Can't quite pull my head together. Long duration of effect. Orgasmic sensations. Total body, mind, and sensory orgasm. What a composite of feelings, sensations, perception, thoughts, experiences.

Wham! Bombarding the senses. Almost too much. Almost. I've pushed the limits. I've teased and taunted death. I could never physically stand a larger dose. Emotionally I'm not sure what it would be like. I might never return. Wonderful. Exhilarating. Incomparable.

I'm being flooded with pleasurable stimuli and

pleasant sensations. I've done it. I've gone where I wanted with this drug. Ten years of trials and tribulations and I've finally made it. The rush of all rushes. The most the body and mind can possibly experience. The ultimate drug experience.

I'm calm now. Relaxed. It was my last injection. I can now finally say that with assurance.

I never knew quite why I had to continue the search. I now know. I've reached incomparable heights with this drug. It's over. Never again will it tempt me. I came, I saw, I tried. I conquered. This may be one of the most important events in my life. I know where I've been, why I went there, and why the task is now completed. I've never felt such peace after an injection.

The mind, the body, the environment, the ideas, and the drug at last come together and harmonize. I've waited so long; yet I knew I would succeed one day. This is the day. A memorable one. A part of me is fading away, but at this point in my life I have many satisfying and intensely stimulating replacements. I can now finally dedicate my all, my entire being, to the most important aspects of my life—my husband, my family, my work. There is nothing to hide anymore. It's behind me now and I'm free at last.

I received what I came for, and it was just what I needed. My life space is in proper perspective. I am aware of who I really am, and I've worked so hard to become aware. My mind-body-ideas are in harmony.

It got me here today. It is the strongest, most powerful, most beautiful, most intense concept man has.

I think I found God.

I wrote this account one early-autumn afternoon exactly two years before I entered Ridgeview Institute for treatment for acute drug addiction and alcoholism. All of it was true—at least I perceived it. The real truth, of course, was something else.

For starters, that September high was not the last time I injected amphetamines. Over the next two years, I ate or injected speed and cocaine many, many more times, and I ate vast amounts of codeine, Percodan, Demerol, Dilaudid, and other drugs on a daily basis. I smoked marijuana the way a casual smoker enjoys cigarettes—five or six a day—and I drank like a trooper: beer, Southern Comfort, whatever was available. I had no idea that the pounds of pot I smoked or the liters of booze I drank were dangerous, and I certainly couldn't believe they were addictive. Whenever I thought my drug use was getting out of hand (a rare occasion), I would "cut back" to pot and alcohol and consider myself clean.

All in all, the denial I exhibit in that 1979 account, which I wrote at the zenith of my addiction, is astonishing. ("Denial" is the addict's inability to recognize that he or she has a drug problem.) I say that I recovered from my adolescent bout with addiction. God! I didn't have the vaguest notion what true recovery was until years later. I say that I used speed solely for task-oriented purposes, but the fact is, I used it whenever, wherever, and however I had it, and I often had to struggle to make sure it would not interfere with my work.

Pervading this entire account is the classic grandiosity of the addict—the attitude that those of us who require the excessive stimulation of drugs are somehow superior and unique, that we have grown from our drug-related experiences, that we possess some secret piece of information which sober beings cannot possibly comprehend. The denial mechanism is most blatant when I say, and truly believe, that I am able to control my desire for this drug. That is the darkest and saddest lie of all.

Clearly, at the time I wrote this account, I had no idea whatsoever that I was an addict. Despite an extremely troubled history with drugs, despite my training as a physician, the fact that I was addicted eluded me completely. How could I be a junkie? I had been an exceptional student and was now an award-winning medical resident. I lived in a nice house, had a respectable husband and a reasonably happy family life. I had my shit together. Moreover, I was a star in my particular stratosphere.

But the truth was that by the fall of 1979 I was careering down a dangerous road. I would crash two years later. Two physicians, utter strangers to me, would threaten to take away my medical license and destroy my career in an effort to help me. My marriage and my family life would be in shambles. And I would enter into treatment that would be devastatingly painful—physically, emotionally, spiritually. The only thing worse would have been death; in fact, death would have been a welcome relief. When I arrived at Ridgeview Institute in September 1981, my doctor told me that I had gone further with drugs than anyone he had ever seen—and lived.

But live I did. Not because I was a medical superstar. Not because I was an exceptional person. Not even because I desperately wanted to live; as a matter of fact, I attempted suicide shortly after I entered treatment.

I lived because in treatment I found people who understood me, empathized with me, and cared for me. I lived because I was forced to confront my addiction, admit to it, accept it, and fight it. I lived because I found hope. And I lived because I found God. Not the phony god I thought I had found in 100 milligrams of pure methamphetamine, but a God who found me, supported me, sustained and saved me.

What follows is my story. In many ways, it is a rather typical one—because the disease of addiction is so pervasive in our world and because, as with me, identifying addiction and then treating it is always inordinately problematical. In other ways, however, I think my story is an exceptional and wonderful one, if only because I survived, prospered, and continue to recover.

Yes, recovery is possible. Yes, there is hope.

2
DADDY'S LITTLE GIRL

sunchild
lovely sunchild
lets insipid figures of light pass by.
sunchild
beautiful sunchild
in an array of colors all her own.
time elapses
time, changeable time
moonchild
glorious moonchild
appears in the darkness of the sky.
MARTHA MORRISON, 1970

Fayetteville, Arkansas, a small, relatively quiet town, sits in the far northwest corner of the state in the foothills of the Ozark Mountains. From a couple of the ridges and high points around town, you can see the plains of Oklahoma in the distance, and on a cloudless day, you might even catch a glimpse of Missouri.

To get to Fayetteville, you have to go through Memphis, St. Louis, Kansas City, or a couple of other towns that are substantially larger than Fayetteville (population: 39,000, not including college students). You take a jet to Memphis, or wherever, then get on a puddle jumper that puts you down on one of the airport's two runways. Most people make this trek to go to a Razorback game or some other University of Arkansas affair. (Fayetteville's main claim to fame is the U. of A.'s renowned football team.) Others, like me, fly back to Fayetteville just to go home.

I was born there on July 10, 1952, the second and last child of Eliene and Doyle Morrison, first and only sister (after eleven years) of Eddie Morrison. Ours was a middle-class family of staunch southern Baptists, proud of our long Arkansan heritage (many, many generations), intense—if not overzealous—supporters of the Razorbacks.

My parents were fairly well off. My mother was a housewife and my father was an accountant and business manager with the local Ford dealership. They were and are kind, well-respected people, actively involved in church and community affairs, and very well known in town. Pillars of the community, as they say. We lived in a neat, comfortably roomy stone house on the corner of Willow and Maple streets, on the older, better-established side of town. I never lacked material comforts as a child; and since my family was basically stable, happy, and free of conflict, I have no memory of suffering any severe emotional problems. If anything, I was probably fairly spoiled and naive.

I've been told I had colic often as an infant, which necessitated much holding, petting, and walking for endless night-time hours to keep me from screaming my fool head off. I've also been told that I drank out of a bottle until I was six and a half years old. As a result, I was the brunt of a number of family jokes like: "Mother will have to put your baby bottle in your lunch pail when you go to school." Piss on them all, I thought, and simply drank from my bottle when I got home from school.

I was the baby of the family and I played that one for all it was worth—and it was worth plenty. I was always, so it seems, very popular, cute, bright, and intelligent. In school I was a straight-A student and perennial teacher's pet. I was also something of a tomboy. Throughout grade school, I played football with the neighborhood boys almost every afternoon. I was tough and athletic, and learned to compete early on—for grades, for popularity, and for the sake of competition.

Apparently, I knew how to manipulate everyone from a very early age. I always played to win, and win I did. Actually, I was also somewhat unruly and rebellious, but I was so "bright and cute" that I always got away with it. Always.

Eliene Morrison: Martha was a darling little girl. Just as cute as she could be. Eddie was quieter, even as a baby. He slept all night; she hollered all night. The doctor tried all kinds of formulas, but it seems she was allergic to milk.

She was always real bright and active. Once when she was about two or three she was out in the backyard. I rarely took my eyes off her, but I had to look away just for a second. In no time she was out of sight. I was just petrified, and I screamed and I hollered, but she just wouldn't answer me. Finally I found her at the top of one of our evergreen trees, and I had to call Daddy to get the ladder to get her down. Another time, I put her out in the sandbox—again, she was about two years old—looked away for a minute, looked back, and she was sitting there, just as naked as a jaybird.

She was always very bright—got straight A's in school. In our church, little children were given Bibles. The Sunday school teachers would line them up; then the preacher would give out a Scripture number and ask the children to find the passage as fast as they could. Martha was always first.

She was so cute. Everybody just had a fit about her. That may be one of her problems. Sometimes we treated her like a little doll. We spoiled Eddie just as much, but he just didn't take to it as much as Martha did.

She was such a tomboy. When she was about six, my cousin was visiting and she said, "I thought you had a little girl." And I said, "Well, I do." And she said, "Well, there are about eight little boys sitting out here on the back steps." I said, "Oh, yes, they're waiting for Martha to change her clothes so she can play football with them." Martha was always one of the boys.

The men in my life have always had a particularly strong impact on me. Probably my most important lifelong relationship has been with my father. I was always Daddy's girl. Daddy and I were very, very close. I have always loved to fish, and this passion definitely comes from my dad. To this day, I still fish with him often. We began fishing when I was about five years old. It's one of my fondest memories of childhood.

He was active in all sorts of community groups. For example, he was a volunteer fireman for years, and when I was little he would take me along to fires with him, much to my mother's chagrin. Naturally, I loved it. I was addicted to challenge and excitement even at a very young age.

Eliene Morrison: When Martha was about four, we rented a cabin on a lake. The dock was about a block away. One evening, Doyle said he was going fishing and he was taking Martha with him. It got to be about midnight, and they still weren't back, so I walked down to the dock and there she was, just sitting there, pulling the fish out. I got all over Doyle for that—for not bringing her home and putting her to bed. But she has liked to fish all her life.

Doyle Morrison: I've fished all my life. I remember that trip to Bull Shoals. I guess Martha and I fished half the night, and I doubt that she was more than three. We went fishing around here [Fayetteville], at a little creek close to the bridge or in some little river branches. She took to fishing right away. She liked the water—she swam at a real early age, too.

I was also a volunteer fireman for twenty-five years. The fire siren was on top of a three-story building uptown. It would sound, and you could hear it from a couple of miles away. Then you'd call in to the fire station and find out where the fire was. Martha didn't go with me during the day, because usually I'd go straight from work to the fire. But when she was six, seven, eight years old, she used to go with me in the late evening. We'd go out, say, to a small house fire or a grass fire, and she'd sit in the car and watch.

Daddy is a rather quiet and reticent man, unlike my mother or even me, for that matter. But he is solid; he's there for you. To this day, I think he is the finest human being I have ever known, and I have always loved him dearly. I know it's a cliché, but he is as good as gold, and he always has been to everyone. He is a fine Christian man and a loving father. I'm sure my relationship with him has significantly influenced every other relationship I've had with members of the opposite sex.

My second most important lifelong relationship with a man has been with my brother. I always thought Eddie was perfect. He made straight A's in school, was a National Merit scholar, did well at the U. of A., married a very nice woman, has two terrific sons, and has prospered as a business executive. He always did everything my parents wanted—something I could not do. He, too, was and is a fine person and always seemed to know exactly what he wanted from life. I respected him tremendously. And I always felt he cared about me.

Eliene Morrison: Eddie always adored Martha. When Eddie was born, I had a real difficult time, and the doctor told me I shouldn't have any more children. We went around to every doctor, and finally one said if I would agree to have a caesarean section and do everything he told me for nine months, he would go along with us. That's why Eddie is so much older than Martha.

Ed Morrison: I remember when Martha was born, July 10, 1952. On the Fourth of July, the week before, we were out at either my Aunt Roma's or my Aunt Cuba's house—I can't remember which—we'd always go one place or the other on the Fourth. Aunt Roma's kids had a fireworks stand—fireworks were legal then—and they would sell them, but they always had lots of extras. Every time a firecracker went off, Martha would kick Mother.

I was eleven years old and aware of the pregnancy. I wanted a sibling—didn't care whether it was a boy or a girl—and was real excited when she came. I never felt any resentment, even though there was a lot of attention paid to the baby.

We moved from Davidson Street to Willow Street that fall. This was a big move for me—four blocks. Four blocks doesn't sound like much, but it was a whole new neighborhood—a new house, new neighbors, new friends. When Martha was born, a lot of things changed.

Martha was very cute, very vivacious. Actually "cute" isn't exactly the right word; Martha was a very pretty baby. Everybody paid attention to her. I had three real good friends when she was small, and they'd come over and treat her like she was their little sister, too.

I was very close to Mother. For the first five years of my life, during World War II, my dad was overseas in the army. Also, from about age five and a half to age eleven, I had rheumatic fever. For months I was laid up and unable to move—flat on my back. I was anemic and required complete bed rest. I missed lots of school and doing things that other kids do. I never took phys. ed. until junior high school. Martha was born toward the end of that illness.

When my dad got back from the army, he worked very hard—six days a week, twelve hours a day. Nevertheless, both my parents spent an inordinate amount of time with me and with Martha. There was no lack of time and attention. Dad did a lot with me. We fished together in little streams and rivers around Fayetteville. I was active in scouting, and he was our scout leader. As a matter of fact, he stayed in scouting for ten or fifteen years after I got out. When he was a volunteer fireman, I'd go to fires with him fairly frequently if the alarm went off around dinner time or over a weekend. I'd just stand around watching, and I remember Martha going along a time or two.

I think my parents complemented each other very well. Mother was always outgoing, caring—not just toward family, but toward everyone. They never appeared to have conflicts. Daddy was always involved in the community—the Masonic Lodge, the Exchange Club (which is a civic group like Rotary), the volunteer fire department, the Boy Scouts. I can't remember a time when they weren't involved in the community. If a widow needed a porch repaired, Daddy would repair it. If somebody needed food or if the church needed help—whatever—Mother would do it. That's the way they brought us up. Their philosophy is: "If people need help, you help them."

My parents were always very good with me, very understanding and hardworking. They struggled to make a home and family, and I always appreciated what they did. We had a very good relationship; they were never unfair or overbearing. They always did the right thing. They put a great emphasis on security—I suspect because they were brought up during the depression and didn't have much. An education, particularly a college education, was very important to them. I believe they felt this would give us the tools for providing ourselves with security. As a result of this influence, I went to the University of Arkansas and majored in chemical engineering.

Eddie was my idol. Because he was eleven years older, I always looked up to him, felt I had to grow up to be like him and live up to his reputation. He was rarely involved in any sort of trouble and was well liked and well respected—very straight and clean cut.

In later years, my drug use intruded on our relationship significantly. He left home when I was twelve years old and married, but I knew he still worried about me. The summer before I came into treatment he looked at me and said, "I know you're dying. Won't you let us help?" I was shocked, but simply replied, "Nothing's wrong. I'll be fine."

I always felt my relationships with women were a little more problematic and confusing than my relationships with men. I love my mother dearly, but it was with her that I felt inadequate and insecure. If I was Daddy's girl, Eddie was Mama's boy, and I think I was always striving for the uncritical adoration she gave my brother. She was the one who always dressed me beautifully, wanted me to get straight A's in school and go to church twice a week. Somehow I internalized this, and the need to look good became a hallmark of my life. Also, I learned early on that I could manipulate men, but I always knew my mother had a clearer fix on who I really was.

Ed Morrison: Mother and Daddy expected a lot out of both of us. I didn't deliver what I should have from a grade standpoint, but it never became a bone of contention. They might suggest that I could do something better, but they wouldn't get angry, and I'd just promise to try harder.

Doyle Morrison: Martha and Eddie were different. From a real early age, Martha made all her own decisions. Eddie would talk to us about things, but Martha wouldn't consult with us. She'd just decide. She's like that even now.

My maternal grandmother had almost as much influence on me as my mother did. Mammy lived with us and took care of me much of the time. She was my security and I loved her dearly.

One day when I was five years old, strangely, the house was full of relatives—lots of aunts, uncles, and cousins—everyone except Mammy. I couldn't figure out where she'd gone. Then Daddy took me out in the evening with one of my aunts to a strange place. There was Mammy in her Sunday dress, with her makeup on and her hair all done up, but she was lying in a box. She wouldn't speak to me or move or even open her eyes. She wouldn't even breathe. I didn't understand.

Daddy explained that Mammy had died, but I didn't really take in what he was saying. As we drove home, I gazed out the back window of the car at the pouring rain, with tears streaming down my face. But no one else was crying, so I reasoned that big girls didn't cry—it didn't look nice and it hurt too badly. So I resolved I would never cry again. And I didn't, not for the next twenty-four years.

I missed Mammy and always would, but it took years before I realized that Mammy embodied security and love for me. At the same time, I began to understand—although I did not accept—that death meant permanent and total loss, and I deeply resented being left alone in a cold, confused world. Because I loved Mammy so much and missed her so, I suspect that the shock of losing her allowed me to deny the finality of death. I grew up, from that moment on, without fear of death, defying its power, challenging it, always seeking to conquer it. I believe that Mammy's death left a deep and profound mark on me. I loved her very much.

But the death of a beloved grandparent is not unusual in the life of a child. If anything, my girlhood was terribly normal, and life was good to me throughout grade school—full of family love, wonderful Christmases, family reunions on the Fourth of July, and vacations. I made excellent progress in school and had lots of close friends. I was school leader, a straight-A student, extremely active in church, popular, confident, self-assured, and directed. From a very early age, I knew I wanted to be a doctor. I grew up in a warm, supportive, financially secure, religious atmosphere.

Underneath, I was insecure. Years later, I realized that before I was thirty, the only time I could remember feeling secure was when I was four or five, sitting on Mammy's lap. This is my only memory of feeling truly peaceful and loved.

* * *

Ed Morrison: My parents had great respect for doctors. Mother, particularly, would have loved to have a doctor in the family. I did not have a bent in that direction—can't stand the sight of blood. Since I have two boys of my own, we've had to take care of accidents like cuts or scrapes many times. I always deal with it—then walk away and feel nauseated. I can remember Martha, though; she wanted to be a doctor when she was ten or twelve years old.

Eliene Morrison: Martha always wanted to be a doctor. We had a photograph of her and Eddie that I can't seem to find. Eddie is lying on the bed and Martha, who was about three years old, is listening to his chest with a stethoscope. Also, when she was a child, we had a family doctor we were close to, and Martha just worshiped him.

I think one of the reasons we didn't suspect anything with regard to drugs is that it never occurred to us that Martha would do anything out of the ordinary. I guess this is one of the reasons we were so shocked—and it *was* a shock.

When I reached adolescence, I turned my back on all the values and morals I had been raised to cherish. I repudiated everything my parents stood for, partly because I was going through the normal traumas of adolescence, partly because I was bored and the psychedelic sixties had arrived in Fayetteville. But more than anything, it was because of the drugs I was using. And when I rebelled, it was never halfheartedly. It was always all or nothing for me. Always.

3
THE ACID SMILE

it's a strange kind of blood
and a strange kind of breed
but it's full and it's happy and it's content
and it's me.

it's a strange kind of blood
and a strange kind of mind
that stays by itself and withdraws from society
and time.

it's a strange kind of blood
and a strange kind of soul—
the sky is the limit and the sea
is the goal.

MARTHA MORRISON, 1969

No one in my immediate family had a drinking or drug problem, at least not as far as I knew. My parents did not drink, and my brother was super-straight. A few distant aunts, uncles, and cousins, I later learned, had significant problems, but as I entered adolescence, nothing in my home life hinted at my ultimate relationship with drugs.

The only pills in our house were my mother's analgesics. Mother suffered from severe allergies and migraine headaches. For her pain, she took Darvon, a mild and commonly prescribed painkiller.

When I was twelve, I started getting severe headaches myself. I began sneaking her Darvon, and it didn't take too long for me to conclude that if one was good, then three, four, or five must be better. Very quickly, my fledgling skills as a pharmacologist came into play. I figured out that inside the capsules, surrounded by aspirinlike powder, were these little pink balls that contained whatever it was that made me feel so good. I would take the capsules apart, pour out the powder, and eat scores of those little pink balls. Later I learned that this was what heroin addicts used when their drug of choice was scarce. They'd break them down and shoot them up. At the age of twelve in Fayetteville, Arkansas, I'd never heard of the expression "breaking something down," and in the early 1960s I doubt that anyone in town knew much about "shooting up." But I didn't need to be shown; I came by the urge naturally. I didn't shoot up for quite some time, but I had the right instincts.

I had really interesting responses to the Darvon—including feelings of depersonalization and out-of-body experiences. I used to take a fistful of those little pink balls, lie down on my bed, and watch myself floating above. I once went to cheerleading practice high on Darvon. I loved that feeling.

I was very open about my early drinking escapades. At thirteen, I had my first drink at a slumber party, or bunking party, as we called it. We carefully planned the drinking, just to see what it would be like. I got comfortably loaded and it felt good. I never felt I had to drink just to be part of the crowd. I had always had lots of friends, and I seemed to fit into any group. I liked to drink, and although we kept our drinking secret from our parents—or so we thought—getting loaded once in a while was acceptable among my friends.

I have always been your basic "life in the fast lane" sort of person; if it was exciting or adventurous, I'd try it. What's more, I'd do more of it longer and harder and better than anyone else. From the beginning, I always drank more, always controlled it, and always drank to get high. And I never would—never could—drink only one drink. This was true from the very beginning.

By the time I was fourteen and in the eighth or ninth grade, I was experimenting quite a lot with alcohol, along with most of my friends. At first I drank mostly with my girlfriends at parties. I vividly remember two particular experiences.

On my fourteenth birthday, some friends had a big party for me, and I got drunk. I always used to like sweet things like rum and Coke or daiquiris. When I got home, I closed myself in my room and drank an entire pint of cherry vodka. I loved to paint pictures, so I started painting, partly to see if the alcohol would improve my work. (It didn't.) After I went to sleep, I vomited in my bed. It's a wonder I didn't choke, because I was sound asleep—"passed out" might be a more honest way of putting it—when I threw up and didn't discover it until morning. I thought this was gross, but I didn't feel embarrassed or ashamed. I simply cleaned it up. Since no one knew, I figured it was okay, and I forgot about the incident for years.

I often spent the night with my best friend, Joanie, and we would sneak liquor from her parents' cupboard. During my sophomore or junior year in high school, I was crazy about a guy named Tommy. One night, Joanie and I got into her parents' liquor and mixed ourselves some Bacardi rum and cherry Kool Aid. Joanie had no tolerance for alcohol; after one drink, she'd be out of it, but I could drink the entire bottle.

Before too long, we were both totally drunk. We went to bed, but suddenly a plane flew over. I began jumping on the bed and screaming—in that insane, boy-crazy way fifteen-year-old girls have—that I knew Tommy was on that plane. Then I stumbled, fell off the bed, and split my head wide open on the nightstand. Because of the alcohol, I bled like a stuck pig and began throwing up all that cherry Kool-Aid. Joanie's mother rushed me to the emergency room at the local hospital, and I can still see all the blood and cherry Kool-Aid on the back seat of her car.

The first thing the doctor asked me was how much I'd had

WHITE RABBIT

to drink. I said, "Hardly anything." He just looked at me, and I was sure he knew I was lying, but he never said anything to anybody else—like Joanie's mother, for example. He just sewed up my scalp and sent me home. The concussion I suffered from that little experience didn't stop me from getting drunk again the following weekend.

I didn't remember either of these experiences until I'd been sober for over a year. In the first case, I was already drunk, and I drank some more to get drunker—then threw up in my sleep. What's more, I was alone. In the second case, I drank excessively, much more than my friend. I severely injured myself, then lied about my drinking. In other words, I denied the effects of my drinking completely. This was significant alcoholic behavior, especially in one so young, but I thought nothing of the experiences, and, in fact, no one else did either.

As I moved into puberty, boys became another addiction, and as soon as I started dating, I began drinking even more. It was the thing to do—get a couple of six-packs, then go park somewhere.

I always had a boyfriend. As a little girl, I had always played with boys, and our closest neighbors were boys, so, of course, many of my friends were boys. When I was in the seventh grade, I started going steady with a guy named Mark Moore. We sat next to each other in homeroom—Moore and Morrison. Mark was a football jock, and we went out together exclusively throughout seventh and eighth grade.

Then, when I was in the ninth grade, I began going out with Arnie Gordon. By then I was becoming thoroughly obsessed with my boyfriends, and Arnie and I were pretty intense for quite a while. Arnie came from a less well-to-do family, was not a very good student, and dropped out of school before graduating. None of this thrilled my parents, and they strongly objected to my dating him.

But already I was rebelling. And already my addictive

— 22 —

proclivities were taking hold. My diary entries from this period (1967) are revealing:

I still love you, Arnie.

Entirely too much emphasis on joining the church.

Who gives a damn about the Baptists?

I need a cigarette,

I love Arnie.

I want to try a True menthol. Menthols leave a bad taste.

7 Crown whiskey smells good.

I will never drink!

I smoke

What a goddamn fool I am.

Why did Arnie quit school?

God, I love him.

I'm so confused.

B & B smells good, too.

I will never drink.

I really like Don. He helps a lot. I can't believe I finally talked to him.

How can I bust my bourbon bottle?

I need to talk to Don again. I'm so damn confused.

That's it! I am confused.

Come back, Arnie!

"Wine is a mocker, strong drink is raging; and whosoever is deceived thereby is not wise."
Proverbs.

Love!

Happiness is Arnie.

No good. He's a dropout. Think about your reputation.

I don't give a damn, I love him.

I'm worried now—no, that's not the cause.

> *God help me. God, help me. Please!*
> *I really like Don. He helps a lot. I can't believe I*
>   *finally talked to him.*

...and on and on. I kept these sort of poetic, fragmented diaries, written in almost a secret code for many years. I was confused about boys—as are many teenage girls. But, clearly, I had a host of ambivalent feelings about smoking cigarettes and, curiously, about drinking. I sound almost as much in love with 7 Crown whiskey and B & B as I was with Arnie or Don. I could easily substitute a boy's name for the name of the liquor—or vice versa.

Nevertheless, until my junior year in high school, life continued pretty much as it had throughout my childhood. I still got straight A's in school and remained popular with my teachers and friends. I was active in the pep squad, the drama club, and the school newspaper, and even had a part-time job at a local bakery. I was crazy for boys, dated a lot, and had little trouble attracting the guys I set my sights on.

I still went to church regularly—Sunday mornings, Sunday nights, and Wednesday nights for midweek prayer meetings. My friend, Sally Johnson, whom I knew through the church and whose father was a deacon with my dad, still laughs with me about the week-long Baptist revivals we had once a year. Our favorite preacher was a Southern Baptist evangelist who came to our church just for the revivals. We can still hear him say: "Every head bowed, every eye closed. Let us pray to the Lord!"

Sally Johnson Bergman: Martha and I have known each other almost all our lives. We didn't go to school together until junior high, but we were at church together from the time we were babies—the same Sunday school, the same vacation Bible school, the same choir. Sunday morning, Sunday night, Wednesday night. We even had revivals, although they were pretty tame at our church. They were supposed to get us in the right spirit, but never really worked on us.

But slowly the changes were coming. I was beginning to question the validity of the Baptist religion—in fact, I questioned all the "religions" that my family worshiped. By my junior year in high school, I'd developed a healthy contempt for Fayetteville High School; by the end of my senior year, I had grown to hate it.

Fayetteville High was a typical small-town conservative school that promoted a rigid, upright kind of thinking, but by the summer after my sophomore year in high school, 1968, the radical sixties had begun to have some impact in Fayetteville. People were beginning to talk about racial integration, the immorality of the war in Vietnam, women's lib, the sorry plight of the poor, and "flower power." These ideas were very interesting to me, even though they were antithetical to everything my parents believed.

By the end of my junior year, I had taken almost every course in the school curriculum, I had passed them all with honors and little effort, and I was bored to tears. Because I'd always been good in school, popular, well liked, cheerful, and seemingly well adjusted, nobody ever worried about me. My boredom, coupled with my growing tendency to question and repudiate the Fayetteville establishment, was fertile soil in which the notions of free love, political dissent, and mind-blowing drug use could easily take root. When the sixties revolution moved into Arkansas, I was ready for it.

Eliene Morrison: We noticed that she was behaving differently, dressing differently. But I thought this was just a teenage phase she was going through. She had always dressed nicely and was very particular about how she looked, so I thought it would pass.

* * *

Doyle Morrison: There was a big change in her during high school. She was much more distant—wouldn't talk much. She had much more dissension with her mother than with me; I could get along with her better that Eliene could. Martha didn't really confide in me, though. We still went fishing together, but our relationship changed.

I was one of the first members of Fayetteville's "old home crew" to smoke marijuana. Early on, dope and hippies were considered uncool. After all, Arkansas was the heart of the southern Bible Belt, and most of the kids in my high school were straight. The guys sported short hair and madras shirts, and the girls wore cotton shirtwaists, headbands, and Miss America smiles. Until my senior year, I followed this code and carefully covered up my wilder moments, the drinking sprees, the questions that troubled me, my early experiments with drugs.

I first smoked pot during my junior year. A friend and I double-dated with two college guys from the University of Arkansas. We were sitting around the guys' apartment, listening to the Stones, the Doors, Steppenwolf, and Jimi Hendrix, and they offered us some dope. I remember leaning back in the chair, looking at a black-light poster of a psychedelic paisley-patterned cat, and thinking very profoundly: "This is great, man." For me, it was instant tranquillity. We smoked all afternoon and half the night that first time. I loved the superb feeling pot gave me—mellow, able to cope with anything. I fell in love with pot, and for the next thirteen years, not a day went by that I didn't smoke it.

Pot quickly became my solution to the everyday headaches of adolescence—the boys, my parents, the church, the confusion. At this point, I had suffered no terrible or significant traumas, but I still felt a ragged, intense pain. I believed I was the only one in the world who felt confusion and pain, and certainly the only one who experienced it so intensely. And in my family—in my entire social circle, for that matter—it was simply not acceptable to express those sorts of feelings.

Sally Johnson Bergman: I remember the first time I smoked. It was in the summer before my senior year in high school—1969. I was driving with Martha on our way to a concert given by some guys who were friends of hers. She and I smoked before we went to the concert, and then, because it was a Wednesday night, we went on to church.

I remember becoming aware—probably through Martha— that something new was happening in Fayetteville. I knew drugs were around. I told Martha I might like to try some. Martha said, "Are you sure?" And I said yes.

Until then I'd never had many close friends. I guess I was sort of shy and cautious. But with marijuana, I found I could relate to people better. I could get high and establish a kind of bond, a friendship. For me, pot was a way to make friends. I liked the freedom of it—the freedom to express myself, say and do what I wanted without being laughed at. It was probably different for me than for Martha. She was so bright, I think maybe pot kept her from being bored.

After a few months of smoking pot, I began using hallucinogens—LSD and mescaline. Even in early 1969, there wasn't much pot or LSD around, but a few kids at school had it— usually dealt to them by college kids—so it was cheap and easy to get hold of. Mostly kids would just give you a tab or two if they had it. God, it was the first exciting thing to happen in Fayetteville in God knows how long. It was different. I loved doing something first, before everyone else—and I loved doing more of it than anyone else.

We were not like the kids I treat now who begin to take dope simply because everybody else is doing it. The few of us who did drugs formed a special bond. Doing dope was different and nobody knew much about it; so fellow druggies became instant friends. Although the straights, the too-cool kids, formed the majority, while the "heads" or "freaks" made up the uncool minority, it was clear that if you had long hair, wore bellbottoms or raggedy jeans, and did drugs, you had ready-made friends.

I suspect the first time my parents had any inkling about my drug use was early in the summer before my senior year. I had gone to visit my brother and his family in Chattanooga for a couple of weeks. At this point, I was sneaking off to the bathroom occasionally to smoke dope, but nobody in my family knew I even smoked cigarettes.

My parents were due to drive out and pick me up. Before I left Fayetteville, I had been going out with a guy named Bob Ames, whose dad had been transferred to Michigan. Bob played drums in a rock band, was part of the scene, and we'd done a lot of smoking, drinking, and acid together. I had written Bob a letter telling him I'd send him a "shipment of hash" or some such thing if he was having trouble getting drugs in Lansing. His parents had confiscated the letter and sent a copy of it to my parents. Mother and Daddy arrived in Chattanooga determined to confront me. They were upset, but treated me kindly. They kept asking me if I needed some help.

Of course, I lied through my teeth. My parents showed me this photostated copy of the letter in my own handwriting. I said I was simply appalled, and I was. Then I moved into a song and dance about how much I liked Bob, how upset I was that he'd moved away, and how I had wanted to impress him. I confessed that I smoked cigarettes and drank a little, but I didn't know anything about dope. They shouldn't worry.

They believed me. They wanted to.

Ed Morrison: I got married when Martha was about twelve, and my wife and I lived in Chattanooga, Nashville, Houston, and Wilmington at various times over the years. I wasn't around much and saw Martha only once or twice a year.

I remember the business about the letter, but I don't recall a big explosion of any kind. There was incontrovertible evidence that she was involved with drugs, but I don't remember having sleepless nights about her until later.

This may sound a little egotistical, but I knew what was right and proper, and that may be why I got along with my parents better. Some people look to minimize conflict, some look to maximize it. If I did something that would antagonize my parents, I hid it. If Martha did something antagonistic, she took pains to make sure they found out about it.

I think Martha sometimes looked for confrontation. She chose to have conflicts to get her adrenaline flowing. That's a rush right there. She says what she thinks, even if she knows it might be better to keep her mouth shut.

I went back to Fayetteville and for the rest of the summer I dated Tommy Cane, who by then had already finished his freshman year in college. He was the first guy I slept with— down on Rubber Alley, the parking lot behind Razorback stadium. Curiously, I remember feeling that sex was like a drug, which I think was unusual for a sixteen-year-old girl at that time. Already I was using drugs as a frame of reference for other feelings. Tommy and I drank, smoked pot, and dropped acid together, but he wasn't as obsessed with drugs as I was. I described one acid trip in my diary that summer:

> *I swallowed the orange barrel at 9:30 P.M. and smoked two joints of Baptist Ford, the best home-grown Arkansas pot. I was with a local hard rock basic hippie-type band. Dan, Chris, and Tommy were there. They passed a fifth of Bali-Hai. Rapping, laughing, and listening to the Beatles.*
>
> *Suddenly I couldn't stop laughing. No one could. It was all so hysterical. The "glass onion"? Ha!*

Everything was so incredibly funny. Life was just one big trip—a movie running on fast-forward. Twenty minutes passed and time dissolved into eternity. Forty-five minutes passed and it was growing increasingly difficult to visualize the others through the magnificent reds, blues, greens, and yellows. Paisleys and patterns everywhere. It was absolutely gorgeous. The most fantastic light show imaginable or even unimaginable. And it was all so hysterically funny.

Consciousness expanding. It all depended on how you looked at it. What you saw, chose to see, or didn't see. You were the master of your destiny. And to view that destiny was in your power, too. If you so chose.

Screw consciousness expanding. I wanted simply to bathe in the fabulous colors, which were the most intense I had ever experienced. Such delicate patterns. The table, the floor, the chairs. Continuous mind strobe. At a very fast pace, but paradoxically without any conception of time. Music ebbed and flowed in vivid reds, greens, and oranges from the stereo. The waves massaged my body, gently but intensely. I was enthralled and encircled by the previously unexperienced synthesis. Taste was nebulous. Smells were too colorful.

Unfortunately I was unaware that the duration of the trip would be more than twelve hours and I was supposed to be home by 1:00 A.M. So I drove home while I was peaking and had to talk briefly with my parents. I could hardly see my dad because of the colorful patterns and knew I wouldn't be able to keep a straight face, although somehow I did. They never suspected a thing.

I lay in bed the remainder of the night, hallucinating vividly, caught up entirely in an incredible fantasy world. My thoughts became increasingly faster, blocking words to explain them. Time became space and it was as if I had reached a higher level of consciousness from which I was able to view all feelings and thoughts from the past, present, and future.

By the end of summer 1969, challenge, adventure, and excitement were the primary goals in my life. How much could I take? How intense a high could I experience? How far out could I go and come back again?

By the start of my senior year, drugs had become more of an obsession to me than even guys. And with drugs, I was sure I had found the answers, like these e.e. cummings-type thoughts that I recorded at the age of sixteen after I had ingested about 500 micrograms of pure LSD:

who knows? who is known? mankind—fools. the walls are cracking. upon death the sunlight beams. nightmares versus dreams. silence drowning screams. confusion will be my epitaph. crying. soon i'll be on my way. i'm just beginning to see. now i'm on my way. it doesn't matter to me.

sex of god, written above from us below—who are below not above everything. under trees lit with neon lighting, in front of the church.

patterns of the mind. fear enters. fear has held on-to everything. fear takes over but we won't let it. soon disappears. i was scared. at times incomprehensible. live each minute and each minute is lived by you and your capsule. time is gone completely. just small existence. everything and suddenly no remembrance. reality occasionally enters picture. painting life's painting. reality so far away and out of sight. realness in nothing yet everything. all so good. laugh and laugh we must. cannot help the "acid smile." happiness engulfs and prevails. happi-

*ness of being their friends. i love them but i love
everything they stand for patterns in the darkness.
daylight breaks. floats before us as all does. sways.
ocean in a bottle as to life in the capsule and truly it
is life. each minute among everything with everyone.
so beautiful. never again reality.*

4
BORN TO SHOOT SPEED

i talk to the wind
i know it's not the truth i see
will someone slow down and stop
and help me?
but one thing is always there
my needle
i cling to
my needle.

MARTHA MORRISON, 1970

Reality, my day-to-day life, had begun to change radically by the autumn of 1969 when I started my senior year at Fayetteville High. By then, I needed only a couple of courses to graduate, and I knew I could get by without studying. I had begun to hang around with a little band of guys—Robert, Phil, and Mickey—who were one year behind me in school. I was still dating Tommy, but I was becoming less and less interested in him. This confused me because I had been so crazy about him, but I tried not to think about it. I was into the "scene"— and the scene for me and my hippie friends meant drugs.

We were smoking dope and dropping acid daily. I can remember sitting in homeroom at 8:30 A.M. having smoked a joint before I left home and taken a couple of LSD tablets the minute I got to school. My homeroom teacher was kind of odd looking. He was a skinny man with a head like a bald eagle. When we'd "get off" in homeroom, he would start to look very bizarre and it would be all we could do not to break out laughing. Then I'd go to the library for first period and sit around for a while. Around 10:00 A.M. Robert and I would forge passes and split.

One time we left school after first period, drove around all day drinking and smoking, then stopped at Robert's house after school, thinking his mother wouldn't suspect anything. On that particular day, however, he had said he was going to the dentist. The school officials had called the dentist's office, found out he wasn't there, and reported him to his mother. When we walked in the door, loaded and tripping, his mother started screaming at him. He just said "Fuck off, bitch," and turned around and walked out the door. We couldn't handle that kind of confrontation.

Doyle Morrison: During Martha's senior year in high school, we knew something was wrong with her, but we didn't know what. She was moody, and her friends changed. She had several boyfriends who were over here all the time. In retrospect, I suspect they were smoking marijuana. We knew they were smoking, but this didn't smell like regular cigarette smoke.

Eliene Morrison: Eddie and Martha were always allowed to bring home their friends. We thought that was real important. We always knew where Martha was going. But as it turns out, we didn't always know what she was doing.

Drugs—particularly pot and LSD—were everywhere. If you wanted them, they were easy to get from the college kids who brought them in from out of town. I was high on God knows what during the national Vietnam War moratorium in October 1969. My friends and I, decked out in hippie clothes and black armbands, marched in protest in front of the high school and the university. As a result, some of the protestors—myself included—were suspended from school for three days. Many others were arrested. During the fall of 1969, President Nixon came down to Fayetteville to the Arkansas-Texas game, which we lost by two points. We watched the arrival of the President and his entourage from Markham Hill, up above the stadium. We dropped some acid, and the whole event, with the flashing lights, cop cars, and helicopters, took on a twisted, bizarre aura.

Sally Johnson Bergman: I did some LSD, too. Even at school. It was a real challenge to take it and see if you could keep from flipping out at school. Guys would just bring it in and pass it out. It was cheap, and it didn't take much to get off. I never really bought any. There was always somebody around who had it.

My friend Robert was well connected with the drug traffic at the university and had gotten to know some guys—Dick, Don, and Stan—who lived in a small house down near the university. One of the guys, Stan Phillips, was already notorious as the biggest drug dealer in Fayetteville. It was from Stan that Robert got much of our pot and acid.

One evening, I went with Robert to Stan's house to buy some LSD and pot to deal at school the following day. As I walked into the kitchen and gazed around, I realized something new and different was in the works. The place was a mess. Pill bottles, beakers, tongs, mortars and pestles, syringes, needles, and pills were strewn everywhere, and a bunch of guys were running around, more excited than usual.

Don was cooking down an orange liquid (Preludin). Stan looked at me and said, "Would you like a hit of speed?"

"What?" I answered, and he repeated the question.

I was already semi-loaded on high-grade pot, and I had just purchased more pot and also some excellent orange barrel acid.

— 35 —

"Sure, why not?" I replied after only a moment's hesitation. Very little went through my mind. I had never used speed, never read about it, never known anyone who had. That was of no concern. It never occurred to me to be cautious or frightened. This looked like another adventure, another high, another challenge, a really interesting drug. And that was what life was all about, wasn't it?

I sat on the floor. Dick tied me off—that is, he tied a cord around my upper arm so that my veins pulsated. Stan brought the syringe close to my right arm and deftly set the point of the needle in my right brachial vein. I watched closely, all senses heightened in anticipation of the unknown. He withdrew the plunger, and blood registered in the barrel of the syringe as he began to slowly inject about 300 milligrams of the deep yellow liquid into my circulation. Dick loosened his grip on my arm, and Stan withdrew the needle and syringe.

I instantly experienced the most incredible sensation I had ever felt—a tremendous sense of pleasure, of power, of elevation, all in a flash. The top of my head skyrocketed. Vaguely, I heard someone say, "I think I gave her too much. Watch!" I could not have cared less; all I could focus on was that feeling. It was like having an orgasm from every pore of my body. My pulse raced, my vision blurred, my ears rang—and then everything seemed to become crystal clear, yet at the same time I was oblivious to my surroundings.

All I wanted was to grasp that feeling with everything I possessed and experience it to the fullest. I had one clear thought, which I believed was to be my destiny: "This is my life, this is my love; I will do this drug until the day I die." I finally began to plateau and become extremely wired—jumpy, energetic, hyperactive. I knew at that moment that I had found what I was searching for. I knew I had been born to shoot speed.

I looked at Stan, smiled, and said, "That's incredible! Can I have another one?"

Thus began the beginning of the end.

I shot speed two more times that first night, shot up again the following weekend, and then began to shoot daily even at school, for seven to fourteen days in a row. I also shot LSD on several occasions. The second time I hit up, I injected myself, and no one else ever gave me a hit after that.

During the remainder of 1969 and the beginning of 1970, my drug intake reached astonishing proportions. In addition to the speed, I ate excessive amounts of nonprescription stimulants and drugs like Vivarin, Nodoz, Robitussin, and Romilar with codeine. I tripped on mescaline, psilocybin, THC, and PCP on numerous occasions. I still ripped off my mother's Darvon, smoked dope before I went to school in the morning, and often dropped acid at school. I had connections with chemists and not only knew where my acid was coming from but the actual dosage. The largest dose of LSD I took was 1,000 micrograms. The largest quantity of pot I smoked was about one ounce within a seventy-two-hour period (about sixty average-size joints); the smallest amount was about three joints a day.

Sally Johnson Bergman: I knew Martha was shooting speed. It was pretty rare at that time, although by later in the year, lots of people were shooting stuff. I never shot anything. I was too scared. I probably took things that were just as bad for me or as dangerous, but I was kind of reserved and not as easily ready to shoot up. Well, I guess I was ready, but I always had— I guess, it was fear. I would smoke marijuana, but to take LSD or anything else, I always had to be in a place where the environment was controlled. I didn't want any surprises. I didn't want anything unusual happening. I wanted to know where I was, that I could stay there, and that the people around me were going to be all there—in other words, sober enough to take care of me. With pot, I felt I could control myself.

* * *

Obtaining speed and breaking it down were simply fascinating to me and quickly became the most important activities in my life. Once Robert and I got hold of two or three hundred capsules of phenobarbital, a barbiturate or low-grade sedative. For some reason, we didn't have anything else to shoot, so I got the idea of making a solution of the phenobarbs and water, which I figured would make for a pretty strong high after a couple of days. I put the phenobarbs in a glass of water, then set the glass in a dark cupboard off our kitchen. Instead of creating a remarkable drug, all I did was culture a practically lethal solution of bacteria. When we shot this stuff up, I got one of the worst cases of trash fever I can remember.

Trash fever, or cotton fever, is septicemia, a bacterial infection of the blood. I had it a hundred times. With trash fever, you get a high fever, sweats, and chills, and you usually vomit excessively. You hurt all over—your joints, your muscles, your head. I always felt as if every cell in my body were being eaten alive. If you're reasonably healthy, it runs its course in about eight hours, and once you get used to having it (and you're a dedicated junkie), it becomes an acceptable risk.

You "get septic" by shooting bad dope, using contaminated needles or other paraphernalia—in other words, when dirt (bacteria) gets into the drug and therefore into your bloodstream. To break something down you crunch up the tablet or put some of the powder (cocaine, heroin, whatever) into the bowl of a spoon and squirt a little water into it. Then you wad up a cotton ball or tear down a cigarette filter and put it into the spoon to use as a filter. You draw the liquid through the cotton into the syringe. Often, as you do this, you also draw up microscopic pieces of cotton or cigarette filter, which are then injected directly into your bloodstream—hence the term "cotton fever."

If you're an experienced dope fiend, you know within fifteen minutes of shooting if you're coming down with trash fever. Because you're shooting directly into your bloodstream, it doesn't take long for the fever to develop, and when it hits, you know you had better just lie down, because you're going to be sick as hell for the next eight to ten hours. There's nothing you or anybody else can do about it—you just have to ride it out.

Robert and I shot this stuff up in my bedroom, and sure enough, we knew immediately that we'd made a big mistake. I drove him home, but had trouble driving back because, by that time, I was vomiting heavily. (Robert was hardier than I and was fine by the next morning.) When I got home, my temperature was well over 100 degrees. My parents drove me to the emergency room at the hospital, and the doctors immediately did a blood culture and questioned me frankly about what I had taken. I wouldn't tell them anything, partly because I was incoherent from being so sick, but I'm sure they figured it out. In fact, one of the doctors told me frankly that I had "gotten hold of some bad dope." He gave me massive doses of an antibiotic and said if I did not get better, he would have to hospitalize me. Strangely, he said nothing to my parents about the track marks that dotted my arms.

I do not recall being depressed during those early months of my addiction, but I do remember occasionally feeling lonely despite the fact that people were around most of the time. I suspect that I realized I was gradually isolating myself from my straight friends and becoming increasingly hostile and rebellious toward my parents. As soon as I started shooting dope, even my best friends drifted away. I'm sure it bothered them that I was hanging around with some real scummy characters. My new friends and I were doing heavy-duty dope all the time, and our attitude was "Let's see how much we can do and still breathe." None of my old friends were into that. My friend Joanie tried to get me to stop doing so many drugs and going around with these people, but finally she and I just drifted apart.

In the early fall, my relationship with Tommy was crumbling, too. When I told him I was shooting, he freaked out. He would smoke, drink, and even do a little acid under the right circumstances, but shooting serious drugs was anathema to him. I don't remember a dramatic breaking-up scene with Tommy, but soon Tommy was gone and Stan Phillips was in. My relationship with Stan developed as quickly and intensely as my relationship with speed. I met Stan, began shooting speed, began sleeping with Stan. It was as simple as that. Nothing else mattered.

Stan was a student at U. of A., several years older than I was, probably twenty-one or -two at that time. He was from the West Coast, and while in theory he had come to Arkansas to go to college, he had actually come down to deal drugs. He was tall and skinny with shoulder-length jet-black hair and black snakelike eyes—a dope fiend right out of central casting. Much later I heard that he had been arrested for burglary and was doing time in a federal penitentiary.

It was Stan who introduced me to cocaine—pure unadulterated, USP pharmaceutical cocaine, the god of all gods. Once I found cocaine, I was really on the merry-go-round ride of my life. The stimulants were clearly my drugs of choice, and cocaine was the king of them all. From the beginning, I had an intense, dramatic love for this drug and would never—could never—take just one hit. I knew I would do anything—I mean *anything*—to get quantities of this drug. I would have killed if anyone had gotten in my way.

Nevertheless, somehow I figured out early on that I could not take unlimited amounts of cocaine. As I later learned, it is impossible for the human body to cope with injections of cocaine day after day, week after week, year after year. Ultimately I had to develop a rather perverse control over this drug. But in the beginning I had absolutely no limits. I mainlined cocaine the first time I tried it—right into my bloodstream. This was no "let's get to know each other first" sort of affair; this was love at first sight, and that passion never died.

My relationship with speed was slightly different, although, of course, I loved speed almost as much as cocaine. First of all, speed was easier to get. In the late sixties, doctors were prescribing amphetamines for even mild weight problems. I would go into a drugstore 30 or 40 pounds underweight and pass forged prescriptions. But cocaine came either off the street or from drugstore burglaries, so we got it only in spurts.

By this time I had gone totally counterculture. I had let my hair grow very long, I had traded in my shirtwaist dresses for tattered blue jeans and T-shirts with obscene slogans printed on them, and I went barefoot most of the time. I espoused the principles of the SDS and screamed my disapproval of the Vietnam War although, in fact, I was never that serious about politics—the social protest just came with the drugs. I did a total role reversal from pep squad leader, newspaper editor, thespian, and all-around American girl to glassy-eyed scruffy-looking peace, love, and drug freak. I quit my bakery job because hiding the I.V. tracks on my arms—and just dealing with the responsibility—became too much for me. I never picked up my last three paychecks because I was too ashamed of my inability to deal with my work responsibility.

I still tried to go to school because that's what my mother wanted. I believed that as long as I stayed in school and got good grades, everything would be all right. This was the most heavily stressed value I had grown up with and it had been reinforced again and again.

Eliene Morrison: I think the fact that she was so bright prevented us from noticing the drugs. Of course, we'd never heard of drugs. Or taking somebody else's medicine, as she says she did. We just didn't think about things like that.

I thought about what I was doing, but my thoughts were

confused and twisted. I would write long, convoluted essays
while high on amphetamines, trying to sort out my feelings
and values. Here are excerpts from two of them:

> Time *is inconceivable; incomprehensible. There's
> always been time and there always will be. Time
> never stops, although it occasionally seems to slow
> down. It can't be stopped. In fact, time is the only
> item that is truly independent. It consults with no
> one and it depends on no one. It asks for no assis-
> tance and continually refuses any interference.*
>
> *Time determines the difference between unreality
> and reality. Time essentially establishes and sepa-
> rates that which is dead and that which is alive.
> Every idea conceivable is in proportion to, not de-
> pendent upon, time. Time therefore seems to be the
> main controlling factor. I wonder if someday some-
> one will capture and tame time and learn the secrets
> of the past and future? Would it help man in any
> way as an individual or in his search? Only time
> can tell.*

> *What should one's values be based on? What is
> truly worthwhile? In other words, what means most
> to you and how much do these things, ideas, or
> whatever really mean? Value should be placed on
> wisdom, independence, individuality, truth, reality,
> freedom, and the happiness obtained through these
> virtues. Happiness exists in a purely free mental
> state, composed of ideas; I must therefore conclude
> that these are the virtues to search for. And these
> virtues are to be valued highly and considered pre-
> cious for they are the very essence of existence. . . .
> What causes people not to care? Is it self-interest and
> a complete coldness toward others? Could the emo-*

tion of disinterest or indifference be so powerful as to destroy humanity? Why does man gradually lose contact and become despondent? What makes men hate enough to kill one another? Why does everyone quit searching? Is it that hopeless? Why does no one care anymore? Reality has been engulfed and almost dissolved by the force of unreality. The illusion is winning. Humanity is losing.

When I read these thoughts now, particularly these notions about "values," I realize how confused I was. I was not talking about "time" or about the "eternal man"; I was speaking of myself. I was the one losing contact with reality and becoming despondent. I was feeling so disinterested that I was trying to destroy myself. I had quit searching, felt hopeless, and didn't really care anymore. My own reality had almost dissolved.

Shortly before Christmas, my parents received an anonymous letter telling them that I was heavily involved in drugs— both taking drugs and dealing them. My parents came into my room late one morning to show me the letter and to tell me they wanted me to see our family doctor. They were doubly alarmed because they had trouble waking me. Later, although they told me I talked to them for over an hour, I had no detailed memory of our conversation. Years later, I realized that I was probably in the midst of a blackout.

Eliene Morrison: We got a letter from someone telling us what was going on—an anonymous letter. We were petrified; we hadn't known it was drugs. We didn't know which way to turn, but Martha had reached the point where we knew something had to be done. When we got the letter, I called our family doctor and told him about it. He said, "She may go down a dark alley but she'll always be smart enough to turn back."

We showed the letter to her. She had been staying out late.

Then one day she just left. But all the time she was gone, she didn't miss a day of calling. She'd say, "I won't tell you where I am, Mother, but I will tell you that I'm all right." She did that every day she was gone. No matter how mad she got, she never stopped calling us.

But for such a long time, I just said—and I know Doyle did, too—"What did we do wrong?" And we kept that up for years. "Where did we go wrong? Where did we make a mistake?" But then I finally just thought, "Well, if we did something wrong, then it's already done; we don't need to worry about that. We can just hope we did something right, too. And I think we did do something right. If we had not, then she would not have known enough to turn to the Lord and ask him for help."

The reality that I was in deep trouble made some impression on me. After the anonymous letter came, I convinced my parents to allow me to take their car to finish my Christmas shopping. I spent the afternoon shopping—and planning what I was going to do next. I drove back home, parked the car in the driveway, and left my parents' gifts on the front seat. Then I went over to Stan's house and, for all intents and purposes, moved in with him. By then my body and mind were so steeped in drugs that I didn't consider what I was going to do next. I could live one day at a time, one minute at a time.

Stan and I stayed together for several weeks. Sometimes we lived in the house in town that he shared with his buddies, and sometimes we stayed in a little run-down place out in the country with a couple he knew, Theresa and Bill. My parents had no idea where I was. During the weeks that followed, I went home only once—on Christmas day to open presents with my parents. All the time I was gone, I knew they were paralyzed with fear, and I tried to alleviate their terror by calling my mother once a day to tell her I was fine. I also attempted to keep up with my schoolwork, although most days I skipped class entirely.

Ed Morrison: The Christmas she ran away was extremely difficult. It was the first time I remember having sleepless nights over Martha. My wife and I found out she had left home when we telephoned my parents on Christmas day and she wasn't there. This was upsetting to my wife and me, and our kids wanted to talk to Aunt Martha. We thought drugs were a California problem or an inner-city problem. We couldn't believe they were a problem in Arkansas.

I had some sense that I was on the edge of a crisis, but I had no idea how my life would work itself out. I was living with the biggest and really the only "professional" drug dealer in town. I was wired on Preludin, Desoxyn, or crystal meth routinely for ten days to two weeks at a time. Although I was still going to school and attempting to assure my parents that everything was okay, at some level I knew it wasn't.

5
NO EASY WAY OUT

how do you get away from it all
how
someone, somewhere, answer me
what can i do
i'm a loner
but why why
do i have to be a loser too?
                    MARTHA MORRISON, 1970

I looked up from my psychology final exam and a cold, paralyzing paranoia struck me when I saw the cop standing at the door of the classroom. My teacher strolled nervously down the aisle, then confirmed my worst fear: "Martha, they'd like to see you outside," she said. I was so wired I could hardly sit still, but I saw no way out of this encounter, short of jumping out of the window.

"I have a warrant for your arrest. Come with me," the cop said simply.

By coincidence, Phil and Robert happened to be walking down the hallway just as the cop spoke to me. Out of the corner of my eye, I caught the look of horror that crossed their faces. *Busted.* If I hadn't already known how much trouble I was in, their look of terror would have told me.

"You have to come with me to the station," the cop said. "Just come with me now. No one's going to hurt you."

I'm sure he was trying to comfort me, but his comment sent my paranoia sky high. The speed coursing through my veins didn't help much. He didn't cuff me or drag me, just took me by the arm and led me to his car. I asked him if I could have a cigarette, and he gave me two Viceroys.

I could have driven around Fayetteville blindfolded, and I quickly realized that the police station was not our destination. I couldn't make any sense of this and became practically delusional. Who was this guy? What was happening? Who was responsible for this? When would this nightmare end?

"I thought you were taking me to jail," I said.

"No, I have orders to take you to the hospital," he said. I would rather have gone to jail than the hospital; at least there I could have posted bond. I knew as soon as we got to the hospital they would take a blood sample, look at the tracks on my arms, and it would be all over. When we pulled into the parking lot, I jumped out of the car and tried to run for it.

However, by this time, the speed was wearing off, and physically I was in an incredibly deteriorated condition. I had dropped 50 pounds in three months and was down to about 103 pounds on a five-foot-ten frame. Six months before, I might have had a pretty good chance of outrunning a redneck cop, but not now. I'd been septic on numerous occasions and, without knowing it, had serum hepatitis. I'd been putting a needle into my arm ten to twenty times daily, and I had been running speed for about two weeks. Also, I had slept and eaten very little for the past week or ten days.

I ran about 10 feet before the cop grabbed me.

Suddenly three orderlies surrounded me and dragged me through the doors and down the hall to an examining room. I had never felt so humiliated in my life. What had I done? Why were they doing this to me? I'd never hurt anyone in my entire life, and I certainly had no idea that I might be hurting myself.

Within minutes our family doctor arrived. I remember his saying that I looked like a concentration camp victim. He saw the track marks on my arm, and I noticed a look of fear in his eyes.

"Your parents didn't know any other way to stop you," he said. "I'm going to help you."

That's all I heard. I tried to smile. My parents had always taught me to be polite. "I'll be fine," I said.

Doyle Morrison: We thought for a while that Martha had probably written the anonymous letter herself, had asked someone else to rewrite it, and had then sent it to us. We were just guessing, of course. The letter was about her and the other kids who were involved with drugs. For some time before that letter arrived, we had known she was doing something. We figured she was smoking marijuana. But this was all new to us.

When we got the letter, we notified the principal of the high school that we wanted to have her picked up. She wasn't going to school regularly, and we didn't know where she was living. When she finally came in to school, the principal called us, and then we asked the chief of police to pick her up. I guess he sent a guy over to get her. We had talked to our family doctor about her a few days before, and he had advised us to have her taken to the hospital in Fayetteville and then to the hospital down in Little Rock.

It wouldn't be too long until she was eighteen and we would have no legal control over her, but at this time we could still have her picked up as a minor. That was all the information we had—and it was scary.

They undressed me and put me in a standard hospital gown—open up the back. I wasn't allowed to have anything—no socks, no shoes, no jewelry, no cigarettes, and God knows, no drugs. I wanted nothing more than a hit of speed so that I could handle all of this. Then they led me down the hall and locked me up in a 6-by-10-foot cell with a drain in the floor. This cell had a massive steel door with a tiny screened window in it; there was a small barred window on the opposite wall. The only piece of furniture was a low single bed. I was astounded. I was alone, afraid, totally lost, and trapped like a caged, sick animal.

I refused to see my parents. After all, they were responsible for this. I would never, ever trust anyone after this. Never! I kept looking at the drain and the small barred window in the door. And the locks. Christ, machine guns couldn't have broken me out of that place. (I later learned that Stan, Robert, Phil, and several of my other buddies had made plans to force their way into the hospital, guns and all, and break me out. Thank God that never happened.)

The nurses would peer through the window, but they wouldn't speak to me. I could hear them having both real and imagined conversations about me.

"She's an amphetamine addict. I've never seen one. You know how violent they can be."

I was horrified. I was no drug addict and had never been violent toward anyone or anything. I was seventeen years old, a well-brought-up southern Baptist girl. I couldn't believe they were afraid of me!

I paced madly up and down, up and down, back and forth, back and forth, unable to take more than five steps in any one direction. Locked up, coming off speed, and they were all afraid of me. Preposterous! "Screw them all!" I finally screamed in absolute desperation.

After a couple of hours, the shrink walked in, a local doctor I knew well. Hell, I knew everyone in town. I also knew what a jerk he was. He stayed with me for exactly four minutes. I tried to remain calm and polite. I simply denied that I had any particular problems. He left and reported that I was angry, hostile, uncooperative, and psychotic. He recommended that I be committed to the psychiatric ward at the University of Arkansas Medical Center in Little Rock.

They had me. No easy way out for this little girl. My doctor threatened to involve the police. I somehow had the sense to realize it wasn't me they wanted; they were after Stan, because he was a known dealer. Because of my age, I knew if I didn't agree to go to the hospital, my parents could and would have me committed. They also let me know that they were ready to swear out a warrant for the arrest of my friends.

When I came down from the speed, I lay on the bed, slept for forty-eight hours, and caused no one any trouble. No one, aside from my family doctor and the psychiatrist, talked to me for the entire two days. Others escorted me to the bathroom and delivered food trays, but otherwise I was totally isolated.

My parents drove me to the psychiatric ward at the University of Arkansas Medical Center in Little Rock. This seemed unbelievable to me. I'd landed in the loony bin. Locked up. Alone.

Sally Johnson Bergman: When Martha went to the hospital, I remember feeling sad. I don't remember being frightened— except for her. I didn't know what would happen with her, and I felt a loss. Word got around real fast.

I was the youngest patient ever admitted to the adult psychiatric ward at UAMC and the first drug abuser. Experienced con artist that I was, I played the "good little girl" game to the hilt. I quickly learned which staff members to brown-nose, which ones to act cute with, and which ones to be sincere with, and soon they all loved me. I was very compliant, bright, and intelligent. My goal: to get out. Fast.

The ward consisted of a central, open solarium with a TV set, a Ping-Pong table, and a nursing station. Small semiprivate rooms ran down two L-shaped halls, and an occupational therapy area (basket weaving, as I came to call it) was set up off to one side. All the windows were tightly closed and thickly screened, and the doors at either end of the ward were double-locked.

Fortunately I was assigned to a young resident psychiatrist, Dr. Martin, a tall, blond, good-looking doctor, and, predictably, I fell in love with him. Unlike the other doctors on the ward, he didn't immediately dismiss me because I was shooting dope. He would talk to me with a certain degree of intimacy; he was one of the first "older" people I encountered whom I felt I could trust, if only a little bit.

It took me ten days to convince the staff that I had simply fallen in with the wrong crowd. I told them I had learned my lesson. I never really enjoyed taking drugs anyway, I would certainly stop hanging around with those no-good hippies who had gotten me into all this, and I had no intention of ever using drugs again. I was good, very good, and they decided that I should return home. They seemed to quickly forget that for the first four days of my hospital stay, no doctor or lab technician could draw blood for routine lab tests because my arms were so tracked up. I was very convincing. I fooled everyone, including myself.

Eliene Morrison: Our family doctor had put us in touch with a young resident psychiatrist, Dr. Martin, who was real sarcastic with us. The first thing he said was "Have you ever done anything with your child besides go to church?" She was down there for about two weeks. I didn't think she was ready to come home, but this same resident, Dr. Martin, thought she was.

My parents came to Little Rock and drove me back to Fayetteville, but I ran away from home that very night to be with Stan. As soon as I hooked up with him, I dropped a fistful of acid and mescaline tabs, ate some Benzedrine and Dexamyl, and smoked several joints. Then we holed up about 20 miles outside of Fayetteville, with Stan's friends, Bill and Theresa, who were as severely addicted as we were.

Eliene Morrison: We brought Martha home from Little Rock in this snowstorm. It took us six hours for what is normally a three-and-a-half-hour drive. She came in the door and went straight to bed. That night she was gone again. She just ran off. She left us a little note, and then she was gone.

There was snow on the ground, and the temperature was way below zero. Like all good drug addicts, Stan and his friends tended to be on the slightly irresponsible side and had failed to pay their utility bill, so their heat had been cut off. We were freezing to death, so we began burning everything in the house that was combustible—chairs, tables, newspapers, window shades, whatever was handy—in the fireplace.

It was cold beyond belief, and I had just escaped from an insane asylum—not the most appropriate conditions in which to drop an incredibly large dose of a psychedelic drug. I took the dope anyway, of course. And I flipped out. I saw my entire life pass in front of me in the ashes of the fireplace—from birth through childhood and adolescence to the present. I saw a great life-and-maturity trip, all ending at age thirty. I also kept seeing snakes in the glowing coals, horrible snakes. I remembered thinking that Freud would have loved this one. After hours of obsession and rumination about my life, I came to the conclusion that if I kept on taking drugs, I would end up a junkie in the gutter. Dead.

Some sense of reality, and some of what I had learned in the psych ward, prevailed. I told Stan I had to go back to the hospital. At that point he went crazy. He professed his great love for me and threatened to shoot me and then himself if I tried to leave him. Life was nothing if we could not be together. I had the strange sense that I was going to die anyway, and summoning all the guts I had, I walked out the door. After all, I was only 20 miles from home and 5 miles from the nearest phone. My last conscious thought was "I really may not live through this one!" I got only a few steps out the front door when I heard a shot. Then I passed out.

Stan told me later that he fired a shot out the back door

merely to see what I would do. He said he watched me as I kept on walking, then saw me collapse less than a quarter of a mile from the house. Stan picked me up, put me in his car, and drove me home. I came to at the corner of my street and was able to walk into the house.

Eliene Morrison: The next day, Martha called and came on home. She said she wanted to go back to the hospital. Since it was so snowy, I didn't want to drive, so I called the airline. I didn't want her to change her mind. We got on a plane and flew to Little Rock.

I was readmitted to the adult psychiatric ward only seventy-two hours after I'd been discharged. I had pneumonia, continued to trip for the next five days, and then came down with serum hepatitis. The staff told me they were glad I had made it back alive. I was treated for depression, adolescent adjustment reaction, amphetamine abuse, and paranoid schizophrenia, and was placed on Tofranil, Thorazine, and Mellaril, which are strong antidepressant and antipsychotic drugs.

Not long after coming back to the hospital, I began to have flashbacks from the psychedelic drugs. I freaked out and began pounding the walls, which resulted in three broken knuckles. To counteract my acid overdose, they gave me an inordinately large dose of Thorazine, which knocked me out for two days and required round-the-clock monitoring of my vital signs. I was misdiagnosed as paranoid schizophrenic, common for speed addicts, and therefore they continued to treat me with smaller doses of Thorazine, standard treatment for schizophrenics. Even after my bad response to the drug, they failed to diagnose correctly and comprehend that I was a junkie, not a psychotic.

Sally Johnson Bergman: We sort of accepted Martha going to the hospital. We were concerned about her, but we knew she had asked to go back. I remember, though, that some people were horrified at what she had done. People did not condemn her, but they were shocked.

I recovered fairly quickly from the pneumonia and the hepatitis, but not from the desire to use drugs. On several occasions, with varying degrees of success, I attempted to get hold of drugs while I was in the hospital. At one point, I even tried to sneak some sugar-cube acid into the ward and failed, so I ate twenty Primatene tablets (a stimulant used to treat asthma), was wired for three days, began hallucinating again, and developed a severe case of abdominal cramping. I conned some of the other patients into "cheeking" (putting pills in their mouths, but not swallowing them) their medications for me, then I'd save them up—Valium, Elavil, Darvon, etc.—and take them. Obviously, this time I made no effort to be a "good little girl." In addition to the transgressions with various drugs, I was constantly and purposely breaking rules and wreaking havoc. At one point, I tried to escape and actually physically forced down the double-locked entrance door. This caused a major crisis and quite a run-in with the chairman of the psychiatry department. At another point, I was put in the seclusion room as punishment for some minor misdemeanor, so I put a number of empty cigarette packages and a bundle of paper towels in the sink and set fire to them. It was quite exciting, I thought, especially when they summoned three fire trucks to put out the fire. They almost transferred me to the girls reformatory school for that one.

When I cleared mentally—more or less—I accepted that I was going to be here for a while and entered into the daily life of the ward. I went to group therapy and occupational therapy (where I excelled at ceramics) and became the ward champion at cards and Ping-Pong. I was pretty responsible about attending group therapy sessions (actually, I had no choice), and at certain points appreciated the uniqueness—sometimes the humor—of this experience. In any case, it was a hell of a lot more interesting than Fayetteville High School.

I had never seen people like this. Only one other patient on the ward suffered from a drug-related problem, and she was a middle-aged alcoholic, the wife of a prominent Little Rock attorney, who often ran around stark naked or wearing a tight red sweater and no bottoms. She did have her more lucid moments, and we actually spent a lot of time talking together until one day she got annoyed with me and threw a coffee pot at me. That little act of hostility ended our friendship.

Most of the other patients were either retarded or true schizophrenics and quite crazy. They walked around talking to themselves, acting out, hallucinating, and reaching for invisible things, or else sat catatonic, staring at the wall for days on end. One day in group, I was talking about my experience being "on drugs" and this little British lady really got into it. She began talking about her experiences being "on vanishing cream" and claimed she stayed invisible on vanishing cream most of the time. I decorated my room with psychedelic posters, would sometimes play rock music, and some of the patients liked to come by to listen to the music and look at my walls.

My moods would swing rapidly, although these mood swings seemed to bear no relationship to the medication or any outside circumstances. One day I would be having the time of my life, and the next I would be profoundly depressed and despondent. I would have periods of excess energy, followed by periods of intense self-pity, despair, and confusion. Privately, I had come to the conclusion that death was "true reality" and thus the desired state of being.

One day, some dust from the ceramics I had been working on got under my contact lenses and scratched both my corneas severely. I was in excruciating pain, not only physically, I realized, but emotionally, as well. This was not the first time this sort of revelation had come to me, but on this particular occasion I simply could no longer stand the pain, not in my eyes, not in my head, not in my heart or soul.

Everything and everyone I knew and loved—my family, my friends, my home, my community—seemed so far away. It was as if all of this had been a dream. I was incredibly lonely and hopeless—I had no place to turn. Life was insane, and I had proved that by being locked in the psycho ward. I didn't think anyone had ever experienced the pain, torment, and confusion I had. For the first time in my life, I came up against a feeling that was "too intense."

I closed myself in the seclusion room, which I did periodically when I felt depressed. Knowing I would have one hour before the next point check, I sat down on the mattress, very calmly smashed the mirror from my compact on the floor and, using a piece of broken mirror, began to cut away at my left wrist. A broken mirror is not the best utensil for killing yourself—it's rather like trying to slash your wrists with a kitchen fork. This suicide attempt was turning out to be more work than I'd planned for. Nevertheless, I did manage to draw blood, and sat there, fascinated, watching the blood drip onto the mattress and puddle up on the floor. I felt virtually no pain, at least not compared to what I had been through.

The next thing I knew, all the nurses and orderlies were at the door screaming at me. I screamed back and began to hack away in desperation. They grabbed me, shot me up with a tranquilizer, sewed up my wrist, then locked me in my own room with a one-to-one "sitter," a nurse who sat with me for two days, no more than a couple of feet away. They all told me that they were very upset that I'd tried to kill myself, especially since they hadn't expected it of me.

They called my parents, who drove down to Little Rock immediately. Nevertheless, even though I knew it had been a long journey for them and that they had responded immediately, I refused to see them, which I know caused them pain. I was convinced that my pain was all their fault. They epito-

mized everything I hated, and I thought they hated me—
especially my mother.

Eliene Morrison: We were allowed to go see Martha at the
hospital. We went down there, but she didn't want to see us.
You know, you wonder how you got through it, but at the
time—it was just like what they say at AA—you just take one
step at a time.

I remained in the psych ward for ten weeks, from the
middle of February 1970 until the early part of May, and for
most of that time, I really didn't want to leave. It hadn't taken
long for me to realize that while I was in the hospital, I didn't
have to be responsible for my behavior. I could act as rebellious as I wanted and get away with virtually anything. After
all, I was crazy. I had access to a certain amount of drugs, and I
made friends with several of the nurses, so I ended up
receiving special privileges, such as escorted passes for shopping expeditions and trips to the zoo, which was only a few
blocks away from the hospital. I formed special friendships
with three of the nurses, Mack, Mary, and Henrietta, hardworking, middle-class black women who knew the realities of
life better than any of the highfalutin shrinks. They brought
me small presents—cigarettes, gum, and stickers for my
walls—and bent rules so that I could stay up late to watch
television or visit with them in the nurses' station.

But my most enduring relationship was with Dr. Martin. At
the time he was only about twenty-eight, but to a seventeen-
year-old girl he seemed incredibly worldly. Most of the other
psychiatrists were elderly stuffed shirts who practiced the old-
fashioned, distant type of analysis. Dr. Martin would kick off
his shoes, put his feet on his desk, really talk, and really listen.
He was one of the few people who gave me half a chance. He
took my experiences and observations seriously and shared
some of his own thoughts with me.

He wasn't easy on me, though. Probably because I had such an obsessive crush on him—and demanded special attention anyway—I was often annoyed with him. I got into the habit of writing letters to people during this time—letters that I never mailed, but kept as part of my diary. Here's one of many unsent letters I wrote to Dr. Martin expressing my anger:

> *Dear Dr. Martin:*
> *You really pissed me off today. You and your damn full schedule. Not even enough time to see your own damn patients. Not even enough time to speak when we yell at you—only a wave. Why don't you just go to hell and leave me alone? Don't you realize that it's been four damn days since you've talked to me? But you don't give a damn, do you? At least that's what it seems like. Why don't you just discharge me? After all, why the hell do you want to waste anymore time with a cop-out and bubble gum–chewer? Don't do this to me. It hurts. All you did was get me to express my feelings and then forget me, and damn you, it hurts. It hurts and I won't ever forget that it was you who caused the hurt.*

For a long time, Dr. Martin was the primary target of my anger. But he made a strong positive impression, and I think my experience with him planted the seeds of my ultimate choice of psychiatry as my medical specialty. I decided that the next time I returned to this ward, I would be a resident psychiatrist, not a patient. Dr. Martin had much to do with that decision.

Almost everyone treated me with deference, and I was the subject of numerous special conferences among the doctors and the other medical staff. In retrospect, I find this both amusing and horrifying. I was not schizophrenic, psychotic, or catatonic. I was a drug addict. But because drugs caused me to behave in ways that resembled schizophrenia, I was treated, both medically and socially, like a psychotic. Drug addiction, particularly among middle-class young people, often went unrecognized and untreated during these years, and the hospitals were not accustomed to dealing with this problem, at least not in kids like me. They did not know what to make of it.

Only a few of the professionals, including Dr. Martin and several nurses, recognized that I was not a certifiable nut but a troubled, unhappy, and confused young girl who had taken too many drugs. What is disturbing is that young drug addicts are frequently misdiagnosed and mistreated to this day. No one seemed to know how to treat my problem, except through traditional psychiatric medication and therapy, but I truly felt loved and cared for, and I tried to return that love as much as I was able to. In a sense, the hospital had become a home away from home, a secure refuge.

But after two months, I began to get homesick. I figured I'd better straighten up my act and persuade them to let me go home. Although I perceived myself as able to control the staff, in reality, my thinking was probably a sign that I was ready to go back to my friends and my drugs. They discharged me in early May, with the instruction that I was to continue on antidepressant medication and come for sessions with Dr. Martin every two weeks.

I was sad to leave this time. I had been there almost three months and had made some dear friends among the patients and staff. I would miss Mack, Mary, and Henrietta in particular, but I would continue to write and visit them. And of course I was still in love with Dr. Martin and I'd get to see him every two weeks anyway.

My parents drove down to Little Rock, packed me up, and took me back to Fayetteville. The first night I was home, I went out with Robert and Phil, smoked dope, drank, and caroused. Within forty-eight hours, I was mainlining Dilaudid.

6

MY WORLD IN A SYRINGE

So I stick to my syringe . . .
My world in a syringe.
MARTHA A. MORRISON, 1970

My hospital stay had done me some good. Lurking in my unconscious were the lessons I had learned from Dr. Martin—that drugs could make me crazy, that guys like Stan were dangerous, that I should stay clean. But these warnings were now watered down by the conflicting messages I received from my friends, by my unquenchable anger, and of course by my addiction. I figured I'd been brainwashed. It never entered my mind to stop using altogether.

I was not permitted to attend graduation ceremonies with my class because I had not finished Senior English and Western Civilization, and I had to make those two courses up in summer school. Nevertheless, my mother desperately wanted me to participate in the commencement exercises, and the school arranged for me to pick up a blank diploma if I cared to come. I didn't. I was ranked seventh in my class of 150, and it pissed me off that they were insisting I make up those two courses. I bucked my mother yet again, refused to go to commencement, and ended up watching the ceremonies, sitting by myself on a small hill behind the stadium—loaded, of course.

That summer of 1970 I lived at home with my parents, and

for the first six weeks, all I did was attend summer school and hang out with my friends. I got my diploma, much to my mother's relief, was accepted at the University of Arkansas, and planned to live at home and go to college right there in Fayetteville.

After summer school was finished, I had loads of time on my hands. Like many teenagers, I slept until noon or so, got up, stayed out with my friends until after midnight, came home, had a bite to eat, listened to music, and went to bed. But there were a couple of differences: drugs, lots of drugs; and a sinister feeling of change that hung like a gray cloud over old Fayetteberg. War against the hippies had been declared not only by the straight kids but also by the local cops and the county sheriff, Bud Locke.

The most shocking symptom of this menacing atmosphere involved my friend Phil. In late June a college girl was beaten, raped, and murdered near the university. Kids, particularly hippie kids, swarmed around the campus all the time, and Sheriff Bud Locke wasn't fond of hippies. He was, I felt, determined to pin the rap on one of them in order to teach everybody a lesson. Phil was picked up and charged with the rape and murder because he'd been around the campus late that night getting high on speed, and he had blood on his jacket from shooting up. Later Sheriff Locke claimed he had found the knife that Phil used. It was all a setup—at least that's what we all thought.

There was no way on God's earth that Phil could have raped and murdered anybody, not even if he'd been high. Nobody had a sweeter nature than Phil. What's more, he came from a very nice, well-to-do family; his father was a university professor and his mother was one of Fayetteville's most stalwart community pillars. Small in stature, with tousled blond hair that was always hanging in his eyes, Phil looked like an adorable little ragamuffin. He always wore a baggy corduroy sport coat with sleeves that hung down over his hands, a never-tucked-in dress shirt, and khaki slacks that were always sliding down over his butt.

The murder scandal was all over the papers, Phil sat in the county jail for weeks, and we figured he was going to get fried in the electric chair. His parents nearly went crazy, and probably went broke, trying to get him off. Finally they succeeded, and in September, he was sent, like me, to the Med Center hospital in Little Rock to get his head together. (Still later, his parents sent him to an Outward Bound program in Utah, where he stayed for many months.)

With Phil busted for murder, I was left with only two best friends—Robert and Mickey. Unlike Phil, neither Robert nor Mickey came from a wealthy family. Robert was tall and very thin with long black hair and a tiny mustache and goatee. His father was gone, and his poor mother exerted little control over him. Mickey was a good little guy, quieter than the rest of us. These three guys were not considered "cool" or "cute," and most of my other friends had been shocked when I began hanging out with them. Until then I'd always gone out with really good-looking jocks. Part of me reveled in their surprise. I thought my straight friends didn't like Mickey, Phil, and Robert because they weren't cool—by Fayetteville standards. I figured that if people got to know them, they'd find out that my new friends were really nice guys. I never had a sexual relationship with any of them; they were like brothers to me, and I felt safe with them.

For the first several weeks of the summer, I drove down to Little Rock every other week for my sessions with Dr. Martin. He knew I was taking drugs; in fact, I told him I was drinking and using dope, although I didn't tell him I was shooting. (I thought if I was only drinking and smoking pot, I was clean.) He'd see me late at night or on weekends, and we would sit and rap for two or three hours. I recognized that this was not totally aboveboard, but then, my fantasies about him were so intense that perhaps I just imagined he had the same romantic notions that I did, when, in fact, he was just fitting me into his very busy schedule.

By summer 1970, Fayetteville was like a candy store for junkies—every sort of narcotic, barbiturate, and amphetamine was available for the taking. By the end of June, I was shooting Darvon, codeine, Dilaudid, Demerol, Seconal, pentobarbital, morphine, cocaine, Preludin, Desoxyn, amphetamine sulfate, MDA, STP, THC, and PCP.

Demerol and coke became my particular loves. I continued to use speed, but recognized that it was the drug that made me crazy, so I figured I had better branch out. Coke, I quickly discovered, was a more intense, more sexual high than speed had ever been. Nevertheless, early on, I realized that coke, like alcohol, was one drug that set up such a strong urge in me that it was not worth only a single hit. I also knew that a coke crash was the most devastating downer of all. As a result, I exercised this twisted sort of control over coke, and turned it down if somebody offered me only one hit.

Coke was fairly easy to come by that summer, and I could and would use anywhere from 800 to 2,500 milligrams of pure USP coke over a twenty-four-hour period, sometimes for days on end. Yet after ten days or two weeks of use, I'd be so debilitated that I could barely walk across a room. So I'd stop the coke for a short while and move on to something else. Coke remained my drug of choice, and later, although my body was only able to take twenty-four to forty-eight hours of continuous use, my passion for it never faltered. If anything, it only grew stronger over the years.

I began using Demerol, both liquid and tablets—intravenously, of course—and this opened up a whole new world for me. I could actually get laid back, nod off, and not give a damn about anything. Besides, Demerol had the best rush of all the narcotics—intense and psychedelic.

With a passion for coke and speed coupled with a new infatuation with narcotics, it was only natural that I got into speedballing—that is, hitting up with a stimulant (coke or Preludin) followed immediately by a hit of a narcotic (Demerol, Talwin, or heroin). Speedballing was the ultimate high and the ultimate cooling out. Nothing could beat it. By fall, I was shooting 1,500 to 2,000 milligrams of Preludin in one injection, followed by an injection of 500 to 800 milligrams of Demerol, or 1,000 milligrams of cocaine followed by a heavy hit of heroin.

I was dealing a little bit of everything except coke. I could never sell cocaine; I always kept it all for myself. Whenever I went to Little Rock to see Dr. Martin, I'd deal dope to some of the blacks I'd met when I was hospitalized. I could get anywhere from five to ten dollars a joint for pot, or I could pick up some loose change from selling a load of mini-whites (Benzedrine). These were small cheap-ass amphetamines, and we would have to shoot about fifty of them to get off, but we did.

Of course, I didn't think of myself as a dope dealer; buying and selling stuff was a natural result of using. I would also take dope in almost any circumstances—shooting in the bathroom alone, sitting around a room with others, whatever. Dealing and using—I didn't think about it much. We'd just gather in people's houses, listen to music, wallow in existential raps, get loaded, and trip out.

Our other primary activity became scoping out and ripping off doctors' offices and drugstores. Until the summer of 1970, my lawbreaking had been confined to passing forged prescriptions for speed—which I always found hilarious because here was this grossly underweight girl asking for a prescription for diet pills—or hiring a fat college chick, paying her ten dollars, and getting her to pass the prescription for me. During that summer, however, I got into the pleasures of burglary.

For years to come, I never passed or entered a drugstore, no matter where I was, whether on vacation with my parents or cruising around with my dope-fiend friends, without conjuring up notions about how we could take this store. I'd consider the layout of the store from the outside—the parking lot, the congestion on the street, the location of intersecting streets—and from the inside—the entrances and exits, the location of any alarms, the layout of the pharmaceutical area. Occasionally, we'd pass a bad prescription in a store just to see where the druggist would go within the pharmaceutical area to get the controlled substances.

If we were serious about breaking into a particular store, we'd cruise by it on numerous occasions at all hours of the day and night to check out the best times to hit it. Then, when we were ready to hit the store, we'd simply break a window, kick in the door, or go in through the roof, which usually had a skylight or a roof entrance.

We also ripped off doctors' and dentists' offices, and this was easy to do for a long time. We'd just, again, break a window or jimmy the door, go in, and take any available drugs. We ripped off one doctor's office three times before he installed an alarm. We'd just kick in one of the little side windows, go in, get the drugs, and leave.

Stealing doctors' bags demanded even less careful consideration, since most doctors left their bags in their cars, and many left their cars unlocked. We knew where most of the doctors in town lived—and if we didn't know, we just looked up their addresses in the telephone book. We would drive to a doctor's house and scope out the neighborhood, checking the traffic flow, the location of nearby houses, and the general behavior of the family—what time they left in the morning, came home at night, and went to bed. Ripping off a bag was incredibly simple. We'd drive up to the house, hop out of our car, open the doctor's car door or break the window if necessary, snatch the bag, and leave. We'd usually take out the drugs and toss the bag.

I was very involved in planning these activities, although I never entered an office or pharmacy. I did the driving, and others stole the drugs. I didn't want to take the chance of being caught in the act of burglary. I figured that if I was caught driving, I would be booked as an accomplice and could probably talk my way out of that. This all seems highly unrealistic to me now—not to mention manipulative and sociopathic—but it is indicative of the extent of my addiction even as a teenager.

Further evidence of my addiction was apparent when one evening some of my friends came to me with the contents of a stolen doctor's bag. They knew my reputation as a *PDR* (*Physician's Desk Reference*) scholar and asked me what these vials labeled "epinephrine" were. I realized these were basically adrenaline and reasoned that, because epinephrine was a stimulant, it must be a good high. I quickly volunteered to inject this stuff and immediately experienced the most unpleasant rush of my life. My legs buckled, I turned completely white, had trouble breathing, and felt as if my heart would burst from my chest. I vomited profusely. Nonetheless, with only an addict's perseverance and insanity, I took a second shot—and experienced the same results. Insanity, this was. Total, addictive insanity.

Passing forged prescriptions was standard operating procedure for us and would remain so for me for years to come. And this was one activity I would do on my own. Fayetteville had only four or five drugstores, so we had to branch out to small surrounding towns. I would sometimes spend a day driving all over Arkansas. I'd take a prescription pad, write five or six prescriptions, go into a drugstore, and ask the pharmacist to fill a forged script. (I could rip off prescription pads in a heartbeat; I'd just walk into a doctor's office, ask for an appointment, grab one of the pads that were always lying around, and slip it into my purse or down inside my pants.) I'd make sure my hair was combed, and I'd wear a Razorback T-shirt. At the drugstore, I'd just start chatting with the druggist about the weather, fishing, or the last Arkansas football game.

The only time I was questioned was in a little drugstore in a city about 120 miles south of Fayetteville. This little old pharmacist looked at my prescription, which was made out on a pad I'd ripped off in Springdale, and said, "Who are you, and where are you staying?" Nobody had ever questioned me before, and exhibiting all the arrogance and narcissism of the addict, I thought: How dare you, you little jerk. But I stayed cool and said, "I'm staying about six miles up the road with my aunt and uncle. What difference does that make?" He said, "I don't recognize this doctor's handwriting." Then I answered indignantly, "I'm from Springdale, Arkansas. That's a hundred and twenty miles from here. I wouldn't expect you to recognize this man's handwriting. Are you going to fill this or not?" He filled it.

I entered the University of Arkansas in September of 1970. By this time my drug use was completely out of control and I was blatantly and psychotically paranoid. I had been alternating speed and Demerol or Dilaudid and heroin for weeks. Besides injecting drugs, I was drinking and smoking pot incessantly, eating gross amounts of Valium, antihistamines, mescaline, LSD, Darvon, and God knows what else. I felt isolated, lonely, guilty, angry—and incredibly paranoid. I was convinced that I was the center of a conspiracy, that my closest friend, Robert, was a federal agent, that my parents were out to get me, and that the cops were on my trail. I was sure that every phone I picked up was tapped and that people were following me. It got to the point where I was frequently delusional; I hallucinated even when I wasn't using speed.

Of course, the scandal of Phil's bust was not lost on me, either. I'd managed to get into deeper shit when I sent him some speed inside a candy tin after he'd been admitted to the med center. The drugs got through, but Phil flipped out when he took them. Then he told the staff that I had sent the dope. That was it.

Maybe at some level I wanted to get caught. Somehow I felt

that the only place I could be safe was in the hospital, even if I couldn't take dope there. Where else could I go? I couldn't stay on the streets any longer. Naturally, I couldn't handle anything like getting up in the morning, going to class, taking exams, or participating in a normal college life. Dr. Martin suggested that I go back to the hospital, my parents agreed, and I went peaceably. I dropped out of college after only about three weeks, and my parents took me to the hospital in Little Rock.

I sat in the back seat of my parents' car as they drove me to Little Rock for yet another stay in the loony bin. On a yellow legal pad I wrote obsessively during the entire three-hour drive, almost forty pages of stream-of-consciousness regurgitation of my hysteria and fear.

Why am I going back? To be locked up, observed, controlled, and experimented with. I have to drop out of school; I won't be able to see my friends. (It will be good to see Phil again.) Damn, what's wrong with me? I do not think I'm sick, and I have no intention whatsoever of giving up dope. I just want to get away from everybody and everything.

The main reason I'm going back is because Martin wants me to. Another reason is because of the hassles I receive from people here. If I don't let things cool off, as much as I hate to admit it, I'm going to get my ass busted. And Tucker or Cummings just doesn't appeal to me! It'll do me good to get away from it all. I just plan to go for a week—at the most, two—and then decide about something.

Still another reason, although I doubt I can tell too many people this one, is that I am carrying speed to the extreme! (Even I have to admit!) I don't even feel like a human being anymore. All I think about is shooting dope (preferably speed) and I've somehow managed to have something to shoot for the last month and a half straight. That's absolutely ridiculous, too! But I love every minute of it. Anyway, the things I don't like are ripping off (and enjoying it so damn much) especially from really good friends, passing scripts, and being so hateful and bitchy. If any of my good friends (including even Robert or Phil) had dope I wanted, I wouldn't think twice about ripping it off. Passing scripts is really a rush after I get out of the store, but someday my luck's going to run out. Seven perfect ones so far. I'm just risking too much, but somehow I justify it.

Wow, I thought I loved speed the last time I went into the hospital, but it's my whole life now! But it's what I want and I guess that's what I'll do till I die. Which shouldn't be much more than ten years from now if I keep this up. It's unbelievable the amount of speed I've hit tonight. Damn. I'm so wired! I'll be speeding my little brains off all day tomorrow. I hope I can get my rigs and the barbs in. That's all I'm asking. That'd really be far out!

It'll be good to rap with Phil again. I've missed him. I'm sure he'll be glad to have someone to rap with, too. Loneliness can cause unhappiness. But then, again, some of us get used to it.

Damn, why am I going back? At least I'll be safe. And at least I'll be with Martin. No paranoia, and no continuing hassles. (No damn dope either.) Somewhere to go and rest and get my head together. I need a guy. One I can relate to, understand, communicate with, really love. And one who does dope occasionally, also. I'd die before I'd go straight. But unfortunately I've quit looking for one, and I doubt very seriously if I'll ever find one. So I stick to my syringe. "My world in a syringe" by M.M. Oh, well,

my stoic attitude of indifference will handle it all.
That's life.

During that ride, I also began writing an essay entitled "Life and the Universal Eternity," which went on for thirty pages. Clearly, I was high, compulsive, and probably psychotic as I expounded on my theories of life and the hereafter, but this was the truth as I knew it in 1970. Notice that I began by writing about myself in the third person, a switch from the preceding diary entry, which was written at the same time. I suspect I was at once trying to make my life "real" to myself, and yet remove myself from the fear I felt as a result of my actions. Here are a few excerpts from that essay:

> *She left the old house with its broken doors and cracked floors. Oh, yes, it was haunted all right. But she loved it anyway. Eighteen miles out of town, not a house within a mile, beautiful scenery, and a perfect place for her and the three others to do speed. Perfect. No paranoia. Only occasional visitors who were always welcome. Plenty of speed and plenty of companionship.*
>
> *And what more could you want? Your three best friends, a place to stay, and speed. Vast amounts of Desoxyn. Huge quantities of Preludin. And more crystal meth than anyone would believe possible to manufacture. She loved it...*

Later in the essay, I returned to the first person:

> *Damn! I have never rushed this good off Desoxyn. I can't decide what I like anymore—Preludin or Desoxyn. It was sexual in a way, too. I'll take speed over sex or anything any day. And I started rushing*

when I had in about 15 units, which is rare on Desoxyn. Wham, 20 units are gone, 30, 40, 50, and for the first time I begin to doubt whether I can hit myself with all of it. Determination and desire to rush still harder win over my confusion. If only I could boot it, but I didn't want to press my luck.

I'd rather die than not be able to shoot speed. I love that needle, that syringe, that tie, that speed, and that far out feeling. I even dig the hell out of the blood, especially when it registers up the dropper's neck and I know I've struck gold. I'd do it all the time if it was physically and materialistically possible. I don't care how hard I crash, how sick I get, or how shitty and bitchy I act. Just so I can do my speed.

I don't care about anything—what I do or how I get it, just so little old me is hitting my speed. I'd kill for it, rip off for it, lie for it, any thing for it if it was absolutely necessary. I sincerely believe I'd do anything for it if I had to. I just hope and pray (and I don't even believe in God) that I never have to. The hardest thing would be killing my friends. I couldn't kill Robert, Phil, or Mickey because we're all parts of a whole. Killing them would kill me. (But then, again, so would doing without speed.) And I couldn't kill Martin, but that's all. It'd be the hardest thing in the world to do, because there are several people I really love, but I suppose I'd kill them if it meant speed for me and Robert and Phil and Mickey. But most important of all—me.

That's proof of a conscience or else I'd feel no guilt.

That's undoubtably the worst thing I have ever said or could ever say. I'm not positive about it, but

I'm pretty damn sure. In fact, too sure. I really hope I never kill anyone: not for speed or anyone else or anything.

Reality is the ultimate and supreme force, but love is the true controlling factor over anything. So we love each other, love our home, love our speed, love our ideas. We love the understanding, the feelings we can recognize, we love perfection, happiness, and tranquillity. We love existence. We love. We really love.

I tried to sneak 1,500 milligrams of pentobarbital into the hospital to help me come down, but that attempt failed. I knew I was going to go nuts, and I did. I was again diagnosed as paranoid schizophrenic, and this time they weren't far from the truth. I was, as they say, certifiable. They prescribed Mellaril and Tofranil for psychosis and depression. Besides being overtly fearful and suspicious of everybody and every-thing, I felt I had finally hit rock bottom. It took six days for me to come down off the speed.

This hospital stay was not much different from the last one, only this time I was physically much sicker. Shortly after arriving at the hospital, I developed serum hepatitis again, and the doctors expressed fear that I might already have severe liver damage. But worse, my addiction had taken a much deeper hold on me, physically and psychologically. Phil was discharged shortly after I arrived, so my dreams of having my friend with me evaporated, and I was left with most of the same patients I'd known the previous spring.

My rebelliousness had not abated, either. I continued to manipulate my fellow inmates to cheek drugs for me, and I sniffed glue constantly. On my first leave, I walked out the door and down the street, panhandled some change, and conned an old wino into buying me a bottle of Ripple, which I drank before I returned, seriously exacerbating my hepatitis.

My parents came down every other week for family therapy, which was standard in such situations. They were shocked, which is an understatement, at my behavior, the extent of my drug use, and my sexual promiscuity. They reminded me that "all of Fayetteville" was astounded that I, of all people, had ended up in this mess.

Ed Morrison: I know my parents were devastated by what happened, but they never tried to cover up Martha's problems. I think all they cared about was getting the best care for her.

I visited her in the hospital in Little Rock. I can't remember exactly when, but we sat outside, so it must have been summer or early fall. She was behaving rationally. She said she had her problem licked, and as soon as they [the hospital staff] understood that she was well, she'd be on her way. This must have been the fall of 1970, because I remember meeting Mr. Brady, who was very concerned for Martha.

This time the hospital stay lasted six weeks. Then the decision was made—how, I don't know—that I would enter the State Rehabilitation Program, which was located next to the hospital complex. The rehab program had never had any patients who were drug abusers, and again I was one of the youngest participants. Most of the other rehab patients were schizophrenic or mentally retarded.

The rehabilitation counselor in charge of my case, Joe Brady, was one of the finest people I had ever met. He took a special interest in me, which was probably the only reason I was admitted to the rehab program, since my reputation for rebelliousness had preceded me. He could generally see through my B.S., and clearly cared for me and tried to help me.

I have no clear memory of how or when my relationship with Dr. Martin ended. I know that I saw him throughout my three hospital stays, but the rehab program had its own physicians, and I was under the rehab program's jurisdiction once I moved over there. Normally and therapeutically, a psychiatrist would terminate with a patient in a formal way, but I have no memory of termination. One day he was a major part of my life; the next day he was not. The emotional bond may have been so strong that I was traumatized when it was severed and simply put it out of my mind. Or he may have finished his residency and moved away. To this day, I have no idea what happened to him.

Joe Brady replaced Dr. Martin as my mentor, and I maintained a wonderful relationship with him for many years. What's more, Joe and my parents got along well, and they became strong personal friends. Months later, after I returned to Fayetteville, and for years to come, I would go to Little Rock just to see him, or he would drive up to Fayetteville to see me and my parents. He and I would go to football games together, then out to dinner, and stay out until four or five in the morning drinking. My parents thought this was perfectly fine because I was with Mr. Brady.

Eliene Morrison: Joe Brady is a fine man; we're still close to him. I do remember that he called me once and asked me if he could take Martha and some other girls out for a beer. I said yes, but I suppose that was a wrong move. They say drinking alcohol is the same as taking drugs. But we didn't know that for a long time.

Joe Brady was not a medical doctor; he was a social services counselor with a specialty in client rehabilitation. To me now, the notion that I would go drinking with him is astonishing, but it seemed perfectly normal at the time. I had my drinking under control, and no one equated alcohol with other drugs in those days. It would be years before I understood that alcohol was as lethal a drug as speed or coke.

In the late fall of 1970 I was sent briefly to a rehab dorm, where I roomed with a catatonic old woman who looked like Whistler's Mother. She sat in a chair all day long, staring at the wall and massaging a white washcloth that she draped over the arm of the chair. I was terrified of her, so they moved me to a halfway house, where I stayed for two months. This was a gigantic old house in the old section of Little Rock. Living in the halfway house at that time was another young drug addict, a girl about my age named Janis, who became my best pal during my rehab stay. While the other patients went down to the Salvation Army to darn socks, Janis and I were sent off to school—I to the U. of A. at Little Rock, she to a vocational school.

By spring 1971, Janis and I were ready to be considered outpatients, so we were transferred to the med school dorm, mostly because Joe Brady had no place else to put us and managed to pull a few strings for us. Of course, this later seemed highly ironic, since I ultimately lived in this dorm as a full-fledged medical student. Though I still had my dreams, my view of the med school dorm focused on the excitement of the present situation—a building full of medical students, most of them male. Janis and I raised hell.

I confined my activities to a few short flings, but Janis immediately began a prolonged affair with a third-year med student who ran around the dorm in a monk's robe and had a pet boa constrictor. Janis and I decided that we, too, had to have a pet snake, so we bought one at the pet store and named it Arnie. Of course, pets were forbidden in the dorm, but since we had already purchased Arnie, we figured we'd get him a friend, so I bought a pet rabbit. And then we needed mice— live and fresh—to feed Arnie, so we bought a batch of those every now and then. Our room was always a mess, with rabbit turds all over the floor and live mice running around.

The unfortunate thing about Arnie was that he got quite large, and worse, he got loose one day and we couldn't find him. The dorm staff was not pleased with our behavior anyway, and when we lost Arnie, we got a little scared because we had no idea when or where he might show up. We kept listening for the sound of hysterical screaming so at least we'd know where he'd gone. Apparently, he had never left the room because one night we heard this loud noise, turned on the light, and there was Arnie, dangling from the bookshelves.

I began to do well in school, but I wasn't out of the hospital more than twenty-four hours before I began drinking and smoking dope. I then gradually began to drop a little acid. Before the winter was over, I was shooting speed.

One evening, I was really craving speed, but all I had to shoot was some imipramine (Tofranil), my prescribed antidepressant. I reasoned that since this drug was a mood elevator, it must be somewhat similar to speed. I washed the tablets to remove the candy coating, crushed the pills with a mortar and pestle, added water, and cooked this solution down in a beaker over my hot plate. I drew up the solution in a syringe, leaving the residue in the beaker, and injected 300 milligrams of imipramine. I got incredibly sick and probably came very close to killing myself. Needless to say, I never injected this drug again and, in fact, shortly thereafter, stopped taking even my prescribed dose because it wasn't helping me.

On many occasions, I would simply insert a needle into my arm and either draw blood or inject small quantities of water. I was trying to stay away from speed and coke because of the problems I had, but I could not stay away from the needle. Simple injection, even without the drug, gave me a rush, an incomparable feeling of excitement.

Eliene Morrison: We knew she was taking some drugs while she was in the hospital in Little Rock. She was real buddy-buddy with a couple of the maids, and I just think she got the drugs from them.

As I say, I'm sure we didn't do everything right. No one tried to tell us what to do or anything. I just think people didn't know that much—even the doctors didn't know that much about drugs. You may have had them in a place like New York City, but they hadn't gotten down here yet. The average person doesn't see the pills that their child is taking—if the child doesn't want you to see them.

Ed Morrison: I don't think my parents were unwilling to face up to Martha's problems. Martha is a great actress. I think my parents saw what they saw, and dealt with what they were able to deal with as well as they could. Sometimes it's hard to tell what Daddy's thinking. But I think they take the attitude "Whatever we need to do, we'll do."

Doyle Morrison: We did everything we could to get help for her.

My sickness was totally out of my own and everyone else's control, but I did not realize that, and neither did anyone else. Still, I thought I was doing pretty well. I was going to school and getting good grades. In fact, I stayed in Little Rock throughout the summer, took a fairly heavy course load, and managed to finish my freshman year. No one really suspected I was doing dope, too. So I moved home again and reentered the U. of A. in September. I thought I'd turned over a new leaf—and I had. But it wasn't quite the story I expected it to be.

7

THE NEEDLE AND THE DAMAGE DONE

Who knows?
Who is known?
Mankind—fools,
Walls are cracked.
Upon death, sunlight beams.
Nightmares versus dreams.
Silence drowns screams,
Confusion—my epitaph.
Crying?
MARTHA MORRISON, 1969

My three hospitalizations, my rehabilitation stay, and my halfway house experience had taught me one thing: people would lock me up if they knew I was taking drugs. I decided to clean up my act, go to school, make excellent grades, and con the hell out of everyone. I realized I had some difficulty controlling my drug use, so, for a short time, I cut down on my amphetamine and cocaine intake because I knew these drugs made me paranoid and psychotic. But I never for a moment considered stopping drugs altogether. Sobriety was not an option; in fact, I'm certain I had no notion that such a state existed.

I lived at home with my parents throughout the fall of 1971, but by Christmas I was itching to be on my own. In one of my greatest cons, I persuaded my parents to allow me to live in a duplex they owned on Fallin Street, about six blocks up the ridge from their house. In addition to allowing me to live rent free, they also paid my utilities. My aunt Tude also helped me out with groceries. All they requested was that I make good grades in school and stay clean. I promised both and made straight A's.

At this point, my drug use settled into a pattern that I maintained for the next decade. I drank on a daily basis—beer, tequila, and Lord Calvert—frequently up to three six-packs of beer or a fifth of whiskey a day, but I got drunk only rarely. I smoked pot constantly. I shot speed, coke, and Demerol almost daily, even at school. I would also shoot morphine, methadone, heroin, opium, Preludin, and crystal meth if I had them, although they were less often available. Fallin Street soon became known as "Falldown Street."

I lived alone, but I entertained my friends at my apartment at all hours of the day and night. Robert and Mickey and I picked up where we'd left off during the summer of 1970. We continued to forge prescriptions, rip off drugstores and doctors' offices, and deal drugs in a major way. If anything, our illegal activities escalated. I was called before grand juries twice and questioned about various burglaries, but fortunately I was never asked questions about any burglaries I was familiar with. Jail was the one and only thing that scared me. A jail sentence would have interfered with my outstanding school performance and my career plans. I was majoring in pre-med and had not forgotten my goal to return to medical school in Little Rock.

Nevertheless, I managed to create a facade that looked pretty good, and I made straight A's despite my drug use. I took my anatomy final strung out on Demerol and had to leave the test three times in order to shoot up and vomit; yet I made the highest grade in the class. I also had a part-time job at the local rehab center, which I enjoyed tremendously.

My parents were relatively pleased. I was doing what they wanted—at least half of what they wanted. My attitude was "If I perform, if I have the best jobs, excel academically, make the grades, then don't you dare say a word to me about my drug use. Nobody could have a drug problem and be as successful as I am." I believed this, and I think my parents wanted to believe it. I was in control, or so I thought.

Meanwhile, many of my friends and acquaintances died of drug overdoses, were killed in drug-related accidents, or got arrested and went to prison for drug-related offenses. But my denial was whirling full tilt. I honestly thought I would never die. I didn't have a problem. Other people weren't careful or couldn't handle it; other people died or went to jail. Not me. How I rationalized all those months in a mental hospital, I'll never know, but I was certain of three things: I had to look good on the outside; I couldn't get caught; and I had to have my drugs.

Although I had perfected my exterior persona, I still experienced excruciating inner pain, but I never revealed it to anyone. Rarely a day went by when I didn't experience terror, loneliness, paranoia, and confusion, and I remained preoccupied with death. I just got loaded continuously to cover it all up.

I'd always had a morbid interest in guns and knives. As a youngster, I liked to fire my dad's Walther into the riverbanks because I loved the sound of the explosion. I enjoyed prowling through pawnshops, looking at arms, and I adored other people's gun and knife collections.

During my college years, this obsession with guns increased dramatically. After my "shoot-out" with Stan, I virtually always had one or more guns or knives with me—in my purse, in my car, all over my house, under my pillow. I was a raving paranoid and felt that certain people, both real and imagined, were out to get me. During all my hospitalizations, I had managed to sneak a knife into the hospital; I never knew when I might have to use it on someone else or on myself. I always needed to retain that last little bit of control.

During my college years in Fayetteville, we also ripped off

guns and eventually collected an arsenal that included several shotguns, a .38 revolver, and a cute albeit fairly useless .25 automatic. It was not unusual to see somebody driving around with a gun in the back of his pickup. We'd follow him home, scope out the neighborhood, then go back later that night and steal the gun. We would also cruise parking lots, looking for cars or trucks containing guns.

Clearly, for me, the thrill of scoping a place out, ripping off a gun, and getting away with it was somehow comparable to the rush from the needle. I frequently accepted guns or knives in exchange for dope. Money was never particularly interesting to me; my only passions were the dope and everything that went along with it. And I thought I needed the guns for protection. Life was getting rough. Fortunately, I never had to use one.

During the day, I would attend classes, study, and work a few hours at the rehab center. Then I would come home and run speed. I sometimes kept up this routine for days on end. I would frequently get to the point where the sun would be just above the horizon, but I would be so confused that I did not know whether it was rising or setting. To this day, one of my most poignant memories is of standing at my window so totally dazed and confused that I no longer knew night from day.

I was rarely alone. By now Fayetteville's hippie contingent was larger, and local friends and college acquaintances streamed in and out of the Fallin Street house all the time. I loved having them around, but at the same time, I would become caught up in my own drug-hazed existence: "Don't mess with me, I'm doing my speed"—nothing really mattered to me but the dope. Because so much dope-related activity went on at Fallin Street, my paranoia level was also permanently high.

Eliene Morrison: She acted perfectly normal all through

undergraduate school. We suspected at different times that something wasn't quite right, but we didn't know for certain. She lived a few blocks away and would come in and out. In retrospect, I can think back to times . . . but we didn't know. Anyway, we were probably doing all the wrong things, but we weren't thinking about ourselves. We were only trying to get help for her. She was very opposed to us, but maybe that was the drugs.

Ed Morrison: I can understand addiction. I can't understand doing things that are socially unacceptable, especially if they hold the promise of disaster. I know she's adventuresome—but if she wanted to do something wild, why didn't she take up hang gliding or parachuting or something?

I changed the locks on my doors to make sure my parents didn't make a surprise visit. I drew the curtains and hung blankets and towels over the windows, covering every last little crack so that no one walking or driving by could see inside. I spent hours peeking out to check how many narcs and cops had surrounded the house or to see which cops were driving by, planning a bust. I had a CB radio in the back bedroom, and I would sit in front of it, amid 70 or 80 kilograms of pot, absorbed in the police department's every move. Sometimes I'd perch on a straight chair with my sawed-off shotgun on my lap and ten or twelve other guns within reach, waiting and thinking, Please don't get in my way. I'd have to shoot you.

A casual boyfriend of mine, Brad Williams, moved in with me sometime during my junior year. Brad was good-looking, very intelligent, friendly, outgoing. He had grown up in Fayetteville, but he was a year younger than I, so we'd never been friends during high school. But we met shortly after I returned to Fayetteville after my hospital stay and our relationship developed fairly quickly.

* * *

Sally Johnson Bergman: Brad was a good guy. I always thought so. I didn't know him well in high school because he was a year behind me. He was always a good guy to be around.

To say that Brad and I "dated" and then "fell in love" would be a total distortion. Early on, we were friends, much the way I was friends with Phil, Robert, and Mickey. His parents had divorced not long before I came back to Fayetteville, and Brad was shuttling back and forth between their houses. He felt virtually homeless, so I suggested he move into my place and he agreed. Ours was a classic dependent relationship—like Stan's and my relationship earlier. The difference was that Brad, his family, his friends, and his background were far more acceptable to me and to my parents. We shared intellectual interests, since Brad was studying social work, we both disdained the establishment, and we loved the outdoors. I became very close to his family, particularly his sister Connie; and he cared for and respected mine. We grew to love each other—as much as two troubled people can love each other. But most of all, we both loved drugs.

Brad Williams: My first clear memory of Martha was when she got into trouble. I was a junior in high school and she was a senior, and there was that big hubbub about the police coming and hauling her away from school. That was the first real notice I took of her standing out from the crowd.

People gossiped about Martha a lot. The talk was mainly about how Martha had fallen in with some really rough characters and gotten herself messed up with drugs. I wasn't into that life-style at that point, so I didn't know the same people who knew Martha.

Prior to that, my perception of Martha was that she was kind of a straight arrow, that she ran in the sort of social circles that were beyond reproach with regard to trouble or serious drugs. She looked nice, was made up tastefully, and certainly her personal appearance didn't give any indication that her life was messed up.

I had my own problems at that time. It was pretty obvious to anyone who knew anything about addictive behavior that I had a problem with alcohol. I'd been picked up two or three times for alcohol-related offenses and I went around with guys who drank a lot.

By my senior year in high school, I'd gotten into drugs some. They weren't around that much, and not that many people in the school were involved in drugs, as I recall. Marijuana and LSD were the first drugs I was aware of.

My parents divorced in 1971 during my senior year in high school, which was very disrupting to our family. I dropped out of school that year, and my parents sent me to live with some friends in New Jersey, but I got into more trouble up there. So I came back to Fayetteville and hooked back up with the same gang.

I remember Martha came home for a while during my senior year in high school, and we got together a few times. By then we did have a lot of friends in common, like Stan Phillips. He was just a psychopath—your typical speed freak with his teeth falling out. He used to say, "I'm no hippie—I'm just hanging around for the dope," but he got into a lot of criminal behavior. The last I heard, he was down at Cummins for holding up a drugstore, and I don't know what happened to him after that. Even at that time, he was criminally inclined.

In the fall of 1971, I moved to southern Arkansas to live with my sister and brother-in-law, got my high school equivalency degree, then went to college down there during the spring semester of 1972. I came home to Fayetteville on weekends, and that's when I got involved with Martha.

She and I were often at the same place at the same time doing the same thing. We'd done some drugs together a time or two, and we got friendly. It wasn't really like dating—I never asked her out or anything.

I came home and stayed with my dad for a while, but he sold his house, so I went to live with my mother and step-dad, but that didn't work out. I didn't have any place to live, so Martha said, "Come on, you can move in with me." This was during the fall of 1972. I was starting school in Fayetteville, and I'd found a job, so when we started living together, it was no big deal. It really wasn't. We were just friends. We lived together, we drank together. That was about it.

Brad's younger sister, Connie, spent a lot of time with us during the first couple of years Brad and I knew each other. Connie and I got to be very close, and she's still one of my best friends. She was only fourteen or fifteen when we first met.

Connie Williams Kingston: My parents' divorce was probably the most difficult for me because I was the youngest, only fifteen at the time. Both Brad and my older sister were out of the house, and neither parent had custody of me, so I just sort of went back and forth.

There's no question about it—Brad and Martha raised me through high school. I received a lot of love and nurturing from those two. I lived with them, practically. They did a lot of things for me, like take me with them to the lake. It was like we were a family. Every day I was at Martha and Brad's house from after school until midnight. Their house was like home to me; I'd just sleep somewhere else. Both my parents were dating, and I felt uncomfortable with them; I was more comfortable with Brad and Martha.

The first time I met Martha, Brad brought her over to my mother's apartment because he wanted us to meet this girl he'd been seeing. Martha was very open, and we had an instant friendship. That evening we had a nice dinner together.

After they left, I went over to Dillon's, the local grocery store, to get a pack of cigarettes, and as I walked in I saw Martha walking down this aisle real fast. I said, "Hey, Martha!" and she said: "Come here, right now." So I followed her out to her car, and when we got there, she pulled up her shirt and underneath it she had a big box of fried chicken. I thought this was kind of weird, especially since we'd just eaten dinner, but we started laughing, and just sat in the car and ate fried chicken.

I remember feeling paranoid about including Connie when I was doing drugs. I was afraid I was going to get busted, and I didn't want to be responsible if something happened to Connie.

Connie Williams Kingston: At times, I figured I must be getting in the way. I'd pull one of them aside and ask if they wanted me to leave, but neither would ever say I had to go home. They always included me in everything they did, except hard drugs.

Every night they had to go to the liquor store and get two six-packs, and they always had a great big giant Baggie of marijuana—that was "the evening." I knew they were doing hard drugs, too, but I didn't realize the extent of their drug use. I do remember speed and coke, but I don't recall any heroin. I would have been scared of that.

More and more people my age were smoking pot. I was known as a druggie, but I really didn't feel like one. One lady in town—a real busybody—told my dad that I was selling drugs, but I wasn't. I drank and I smoked pot, but I never did hard drugs and I never dealt them.

During my junior year in college I applied for early admittance to medical school and was accepted as an alternate—that is, I was put on a sort of waiting list. At this point, my parents announced that they would refuse to pay my way through medical school unless Brad and I got married. They felt that we were "living in sin." I had no interest in getting married, never did. Brad and I had lived together for a year, and we were perfectly happy with that arrangement. Neither of us cared much about being married. I loved Brad, but I was focused on going to medical school and sustaining my present life-style. Brad was a part of that life-style, so we succumbed to the pressure and got married in July 1973.

The wedding was no big deal. We decided on a Monday to go ahead with it, and we got married on the following Thursday on the deck of a friend's house overlooking a beautiful valley. Just our families were present. It was really quite nice— and we all got drunk to celebrate.

Brad Williams: Getting married was no big deal. It was not a major commitment. It just seemed like the thing to do. The years we spent together—living together or married—I could summarize in two statements: We went to school, and we got high. That was it. That was all we did.

Ed Morrison: We weren't unhappy about Martha's marriage to Brad. In fact, I thought it was a change toward normalcy. I liked Brad—he's very articulate, very nice. Of course, at that time, I had a burr haircut while Brad had long hair and a mustache; I had a hard time finding that acceptable. I always thought he was a nice fellow, but maybe I didn't feel quite as comfortable with him as I would have with somebody who was more like me.

We wanted to believe that everything was okay. We visited them when they were living in the duplex on Fallin Street. Martha had a garden, and we thought Boy, that looks normal, and we hoped that it was. You have to remember—I wasn't around very much. I'd see her only a few hours at a time, a couple of times a year.

* * *

Even though Brad and I were married, our life-style did not change one bit. We went to school, we worked, we saw our friends and family, and we did drugs. That was it.

Brad Williams: I drank every day—alcohol was my drug of choice and always gave me my worst problems. I liked other drugs, too, and when they were available and we had the money, I took them. But any drug other than alcohol was just a diversion.

I was very dependent on Martha. Any feelings and emotions that weren't drugged were centered on her, on our life together, and on maintaining our life-style. I never really thought about what life would be like after we got out of school. We didn't talk about having a family because we'd pretty much decided not to. At that time, I didn't think I'd live past the age of thirty-five. I was just living one day at a time—getting high today. That was really all there was to it. I was so immature. I just needed somebody.

Martha's parents were very nice to me, always very supportive. Whatever Martha wanted, they would try to help her get it. She wanted me at that time, so that was fine with them.

My own parents knew they couldn't control me, so they closed their eyes. They got involved in a parents' group when I was in high school, but once Martha and I were married, I think they were shed of responsibility as far as I was concerned.

I had my drinking and drugging pretty much under control, I never missed a day of school, and I didn't interrupt my productive involvements. I strived to keep this front going.

During my senior year in college, I reapplied to the University of Arkansas Medical School in Little Rock, the same place where I had been hospitalized four years before. I convinced the admissions committee that I was serious about medicine. I had a 3.6 grade average, with a major in psychology and a minor in chemistry. I had completed all my pre-med course work and had worked at the rehab center and later at the Veterans Hospital in Fayetteville, so it wasn't difficult for them to accept my passion for medicine. I also assured them that I'd cleaned up my act. In fact, I think my hospitalizations worked as a plus rather than a minus. As always, I looked and sounded sincere—I knew what I was talking about.

In August 1974, Brad and I held a garage sale and sold most of our possessions. We made $450 and I spent almost all of it on Demerol. We packed up what we needed and moved to Little Rock. By September I was finally on my way to a medical career.

8
THE MAKING OF A JUNKIE DOCTOR

I never wanted to be a drug addict;
All I ever wanted to be was a doctor.
MARTHA MORRISON, 1982

For the first two years of medical school, Brad and I lived in an apartment in the same med center dorm where I had lived three years before while in outpatient treatment. I quickly realized that for the first time in my life I would actually have to study to make A's, and this was not only a shock but a blow to my ego as well. What's more, studying interfered with my drug use, so I settled for B's and C's.

For us, life in Little Rock was virtually identical to life in Fayetteville—consisting primarily of school and getting high. Brad finished his last year of undergraduate school in Little Rock, then began work on his master's degree in social work. We had many friends in Little Rock, many of whom had come down from Fayetteville, like us, to go to school. Brad's older sister and her husband lived nearby, and in 1975, Brad's younger sister, Connie, got married and moved to Little Rock as well.

Brad Williams: When we moved to Little Rock in 1974, our relationship didn't change right away, but over time it did. Martha became involved with the whole scene at the medical school, and we got involved with different sets of people.

* * *

Connie Williams Kingston: I graduated from high school in 1974, right before Brad and Martha moved to Little Rock. I had met my soon-to-be husband, Mike, who is from Chicago, and attached myself to him—I was eighteen and he was twenty-four. We moved to Little Rock because my brother and sister were there and because we wanted to get out of Fayette- ville. Mike and I got married in 1975.

Brad and Martha were having some troubles. They were violent sometimes. They had a fight at my husband's bachelor party, which was held at a Holiday Inn in Fayetteville. They broke a table and threw a TV set on the floor. We had to pull them apart.

By this time, the rest of my family was starting to stay away from them. Every weekend, Mike and I would go over to their place. Brad and Martha would be sacked out on the convert- ible sofa, so loaded they couldn't move. You'd hit the week- end, and you knew Brad and Martha would be gone.

My drug life remained much the same. I drank and smoked pot daily. If anything, my drinking increased, partly because it was Brad's drug of choice, but more because it was socially acceptable, particularly among the other med students, who were big drinkers. I stopped doing acid because I was afraid I wouldn't come down; at some level, I guess I knew my grasp on reality was tenuous at best. But I continued to shoot coke, heroin, Dilaudid, and Demerol whenever I could afford it and fit it in between the demands and stresses of medical school.

I still took the same "acceptable risks" with septicemia and overdoses. During my sophomore year in med school, I suf- fered one of the worst overdoses I would ever experience.

One evening I went over to Jake Farrow's apartment to buy heroin while Brad stayed in the dorm studying. Jake was an old friend and dope dealer who was also from Fayetteville and had known us for years. Jake assured me that this was dynamite junk and cautioned me about using too much. He was aware that my tolerance level had decreased slightly because I hadn't shot any junk in two or three weeks. Every batch of heroin is different, and you don't know until you actually use it how pure or impure it is.

The first time I did heroin, back in Fayetteville, I thought, This is it! Here I am shooting heroin—this is the big one. As a matter of fact, heroin isn't a big high. It's not that instantaneous *whoa!* you get with speed or coke. No wham, bam, blow-your-head-off as soon as you shoot up. With heroin, it takes a short while to get off, to feel the effects. You can clean up a bit, wash the needle, then mosey into the other room and sit down. You nod out, nothing bothers you, and you go into a dreamlike state. I didn't use heroin for the rush, but for the long-term mellow free-of-all-pain effect.

If you shoot it intramuscularly, you get about the same effect as shooting intravenously, but it's even slower and lasts longer. As a result, I would often shoot myself in the ass. This also was useful for avoiding track marks on my arms.

Jake, the dealer from whom I bought the stuff, was somewhat of an expert on heroin—an experienced junkie who shot up almost every day—so I trusted his judgment. I bought four large hits from him.

Narcotics depress respiration, so I knew I had to be careful or I might stop breathing. Since I hadn't been shooting for a while, I should have done a small hit first to get my tolerance back up. Then I could have gone ahead and shot a shitload on the second or third hit. With all my experience, I should have known better than to use so much in the first injection. I don't recall being overtly suicidal, but I did realize that I was planning to use too much. I suspect my denial was just so strong that I figured nothing would ever happen to me.

I broke all of the heroin down and shot it up intravenously right there in Jake's apartment—all four hits at once. I dropped like a leaf. The next thing I remember, it was about three hours later and Jake was standing over me, obviously in a panic. I'd never seen him like that before. I was lying on his bed, and he screamed, "Get up, I'm taking you home."

I said, "What for? I drove over here; I can drive home!"

He started cussing me out and said, "Don't you know what happened?" He told me I had overdosed and he'd been pumping on my chest and breathing for me for almost three hours. He said he came into the room and found me just lying there—no heartbeat, no breathing, and totally blue.

He put me into his car and drove me home. I was sick for a week—vomiting, headachy. I could hardly move and felt as if I was dying. For years, that was my impression of this experience, and as a result, my denial and my grandiosity soared: I'd beaten death.

After this OD experience, it did occur to me that perhaps I took drugs in a little different fashion than other people did. It never dawned on me to stop, but I did consider cutting down. In the end, though, that's all I did—consider it. Also, heroin became more expensive and of increasingly dubious quality in our part of the country. So I quit doing heroin altogether.

About a year after Jake saved my life, he got busted for breaking into a drugstore in Little Rock, and the cops shot him up pretty badly. Ironically, I was working on the surgical floor where he was hospitalized, and I helped treat him. He went to prison after that.

Over the next two years Brad's alcoholism increased dramatically and he became increasingly irresponsible. Although we loved each other, our relationship had always been tumultuous. Also, as I progressed in med school, we began to grow away from each other, and I'm sure that upset him. I was beginning to excel in my studies, I was obsessed with my work and my career, I was impressing some of the professors, and I worried that Brad and his uncontrollable drinking would hold me back. His drinking was getting out of hand; mine was under control, or so I thought.

During my sophomore year in medical school, I began working in the physiology lab for one of the professors, Paul Frederick. The following summer he and I went to a conference in California. Although I did not begin an affair with him at that time, I did realize that he was interested in me romantically.

When I returned from California, I found that Brad's behavior had gotten even more out of hand. He'd graduated from school and was just lying around, not working or even looking for a job. I was furious at him, and I'm sure he noticed. During one binge, he threatened my dogs, Lhasa and Napoleon. My dogs were like my children to me, and I flat out could not tolerate the thought of violence toward them. This was just the nudge I needed, and, in August 1976, I filed for divorce.

Brad Williams: I thought our divorce was sudden. She went away with Paul on this research trip to California, came back, and a couple of weeks later we split up. I didn't know what had happened. I asked her if she was seeing Paul or somebody else, but she wouldn't tell me, and nobody in my family would tell me anything. It was really baffling to me. Then, about a year later, I found out she'd married Paul.

While she was in California, I had gotten my master's degree, but I hadn't really started looking for a job. When she got back, I was just lying around, drinking. I'd just gotten out of school, and I felt like just killing the summer.

There was a distance between us that hadn't been there before. She was cold. I knew something was wrong. We talked a few times, and she said: "You haven't bothered to get a job. All you're doing is drinking all the time."

We had a couple of fights, and after one of them, she left. I just internalized it all. I knew I was drunk much of the time, but I didn't think I was any worse than I'd ever been. She filed, and we were divorced within sixty days. We saw each other only a few times after that; it was a clean break. I was upset over the break for a long time, but I was real sick, too. I was real sad the whole thing happened and I didn't understand.

After we divorced, I moved into an apartment with a friend and got a job. My drinking got real bad. I quit that job, worked in construction for a while, moved back to Fayetteville, then to Memphis. Then I started going in and out of treatment centers. I was drinking, mostly, but sometimes I'd take pills.

From my point of view, Brad's drinking intruded into my professional life. After I came back from California, I was about to begin my junior year in med school, and I got selfish. I was afraid his drinking would reflect negatively on me in medical school, and I couldn't tolerate that.

Brad Williams: Dependency was the primary force driving that relationship from my perspective. I was shocked when Martha left. My whole life was wrapped around that relationship and keeping that whole life-style going. Many of my feelings of well-being were wrapped up in that relationship.

At the same time, I don't think there would have been any attachment if it hadn't been for our life-style. That was the glue that held us together. Martha and I were friends, and we should have stayed friends. I don't think there was any way for a relationship to develop beyond that point, given the effects of her drugs and my alcohol. We had common interests, but I think the attachment was based on our need to maintain our life-style, and for a long time we could do that better together than we could apart.

Connie Williams Kingston: Today they both look back at their marriage from a sober standpoint. Everything in their lives was affected by drugs and alcohol, but there was a lot of day-to-day stuff that they went through and helped me through that didn't have anything to do with drugs.

When they divorced in 1976, I was upset—it was like my other set of parents had divorced. Mike and I saw more of Martha than we did of Brad after the split. Those were hard years. It was before we knew about Al-Anon, and we didn't know how to act around Brad. What we were doing mostly was feeding his alcoholism. I don't want to say we were "enabling," but we did try to fix everything when Brad was drinking.

We never felt we had to take sides with either Brad or Martha. Martha was part of the family. I really wasn't keen on the idea of having Paul Frederick around, but we did the best we could and tried to get to know him a little better.

I knew that Martha and Brad had been taking drugs, but Martha looked better. Brad's drinking was more visible than her drug use. I would have been dumbfounded if anybody had told me she was addicted to anything. "Addicted" is such a heavy word.

Probably because of my career and the new friends I'd met through med school and work, my feelings about our marriage were different from Brad's. I was probably less dependent on him than he was on me, partly because I had more of a focus to my life. And by then I'd become interested in Paul.

Both of our families and all of our friends supported me when I decided to divorce Brad. Everyone believed he was the one with the problem. Somehow, at that time, I was able to control my public behavior better. And as long as no one knew about my violent episodes, my overdoses, my excesses, then they might as well not have occurred, as far as I was concerned. In retrospect, I'm sure we were both as sick with the illness of co-dependency as we were with chemical dependence. But at the time, I did not know he was sick; I did not know I was sick. Once again, I took advantage of others for the sake of my addiction, and I used everybody and everything in order to go to medical school and excel in the eyes of the world. My life was my drugs and my medical career.

As soon as Brad and I separated, my relationship with Paul intensified. He was more than thirty years older than I, recently divorced, and had the kind of sophistication and offered the kind of support I wanted and needed. If Brad's behavior had been detrimental to my career, Paul—a full professor in the medical school, an internationally respected physiologist, and a settled middle-aged man—could do everything to make me look like a vision of perfection. Marriage to him allowed me to appear to be a gifted medical student, a loving wife, and ultimately, the ideal doctor.

We were married in December 1976, just four months after my divorce from Brad, even though I didn't really want to marry again—or so I thought.

Unconsciously, though, I suppose I looked to Paul to save me, to be a real father figure. When I was just coming off my marriage to Brad, Paul was very attractive to me. Brad had been dependent on me; now I could lean on Paul. He could take control, organize the house, pay the bills, and be responsible for both of us. But I came to discover that being taken care of had its disadvantages. The one who does the caretaking can become possessive, obsessive, jealous, and overly controlling. A healthy, well-balanced relationship this was not. But I didn't know that at the time and, I suspect, neither did he.

Sally Johnson Bergman. I could definitely see the difference between Brad and Paul. Brad was irresponsible. Paul was very organized, and I thought he might be good for Martha.

In the beginning, I really thought I was in love with Paul; I was entranced by him. He was much older and more mature than I was. He was a brilliant man, with a wealth of information and knowledge. He took me to fancy restaurants and spent lots of money on me. I had never been to such places or been treated so nicely. The best part of our marriage was the travel. We went hiking and camping in the Canadian Rockies, the Sierra Nevada, all over California, and in the southwestern deserts. We also made two extended trips to Europe, which opened up a whole new world for me.

But quickly our marriage turned stale and hollow. He was very intellectual and research-oriented; I was very people-oriented. We were both obsessive, but our compulsions took different forms, and thus we often clashed. We had very little in common except our dependent need for each other, and our co-dependency ultimately killed any affection we had for each other. This all became clear within a few short months, but we stayed married for five years.

Connie Williams Kingston: For Martha and Paul to be romantically involved was kind of a surprise, good gossip for a while. Then we all decided it was something she'd grow out of after a while. We were just hoping it would be soon.

I saw Paul as this little bumblebee, moving around all the time, cleaning up something or trying to make things right. When I picture him in my head, he's talking fast, cleaning something up as he talks.

I never felt comfortable in their house. Things had to be too clean. I couldn't go get an ashtray, I didn't feel I could go get myself something to drink. The minute you hit the door, Paul would ask you to take off your shoes.

Paul and I used to have terrible fights about forcing people to take off their shoes before they came into the house. I'd wear my shoes wherever I wanted to, and I couldn't stand him telling my friends to take their shoes off. On top of that, he was always telling me I was the most wasteful person he'd ever met, which was probably true.

Connie Williams Kingston: I remember one time we were making drinks. Martha had a brand-new refrigerator, and I said, "Martha, why don't you use your ice maker?" But she said, "Paul won't let me use it because it wastes too much electricity." We got into this conversation about wasting things, and Paul got on Martha about wasting toothpaste and Coca-Cola. He said she wasted about ten ounces of Coca-Cola every night before she went to bed.

Eliene Morrison: It's hard to dislike anybody—at least, for me it is—and I liked Paul. He was quite a bit older than Martha, but he was very nice, very likable. But he was very frugal and I had a difficult time relating to this. He seemed to dwell on many insignificant and trivial things.

Ed Morrison: Paul was so much older than Martha, and the combination of his accent and his philosophy (he was very opinionated—there was not much room for discussion) made him appear to be a sort of strange individual. But he was well read, well traveled, and interesting.

One time, he took my boys and me down to his laboratory where they were doing experiments on cats. They'd open up the cats' brains, put electrodes on, inject the cats with drugs, then monitor their responses. This was real interesting, but I guess I wasn't cut out to be a doctor. It made me sort of nauseated.

As far as I knew, things were going well with Paul and Martha, and he always seemed to treat her well. Certainly there was no obvious physical or verbal abuse. Martha sometimes dominated, insisting on doing things with or without him—Martha does what Martha wants to do. But he didn't seem to mind that she had a mind of her own.

I continued to use drugs excessively, of course. After all, Paul and I lived together, were married, and my attitude was "Take me, take my drugs." But I continued to perform well; in fact, once we were married and I operated from a firm base, my performance was better than ever. I'm sure it was exceedingly difficult for him to realize I was addicted, despite my excessive drug use, because I performed so well. I felt driven to be the best at everything I did—and if I wasn't the best, I wouldn't do it.

I smoked pot first thing in the morning and last thing at night before going to bed. I ate pills—usually codeine—throughout the day. I drank huge quantities of Lord Calvert, Southern Comfort, and beer every evening. Day in and day out. I shot dope whenever I could, when it didn't interfere with my medical responsibilities.

I threw up every time I injected a large quantity of dope, whether it was a stimulant or a narcotic. I thought this was normal and to be expected. I experienced sporadic fevers, bouts of diarrhea, pain in my joints, constant headaches, and occasional periods of memory loss. I considered this normal, although by this time I was highly trained in physiology and medicine. My tolerance was exceptional: I took in thousands of milligrams of stimulants, hundreds of milligrams of narcotics and barbiturates, ounces and ounces of pot, and liters of liquor. Clearly, I was deteriorating physically and emotionally, but I was sure that I didn't have a problem. No, not me!

Doyle Morrison: I went down to Little Rock several times while Martha was in medical school. She and I would go down to the river and fish. We also went to the races at Hot Springs—she liked that a lot. But we talked only about fishing or racing. There was no conversation about anything personal.

For several years we didn't think she had a drug problem. Sometimes I thought she might have an alcohol problem, but then she would just be herself.

Ed Morrison: When Martha was in medical school, my

parents and I thought she had a drinking problem. We talked about it—but since drinking is more or less acceptable socially, we thought, Thank God it's not drugs.

I was doing exceptionally well in school. I received evaluations like the following: "displays unique scientific scrutiny and has made substantial research contributions in the medical field"; "superior"; "displays those qualities most important in a physician, shows concern for her patients"; "good teacher, great capacity for concentration, remarkable person, bright and lively, intellectually outstanding, possesses great energy and drive, truly superior"; "outstanding ability, tremendous potential, conscientious toward work and admirably compassionate toward patients, exceptional promise."

I received almost all honors during my last two years in medical school, got along well with the other students, nurses, doctors, and was super-responsible at work, conscientious, and dedicated. I knew how to compete, wanted to be the best, and generally was.

I was awarded the Upjohn Achievement Award, a national honor given to a medical student for outstanding research, and published numerous scientific articles before I graduated from med school. I was one of ten people in my graduating class nominated for the Senior Buchanan Key, an award given to those who earn the highest percentage of honors during the senior year and who demonstrate the attributes most desirable in a physician of quality.

I received my M.D. from the University of Arkansas Medical Science Campus in May 1978; I thought my degree meant "M.Deity," not M.D. I passed all my licensing exams with flying colors. I was interested in pursuing psychiatry as my medical specialty, but during my senior year, I had exhibited a flare for and an interest in surgery and decided I should explore surgery and internal medicine further during my internship to see if perhaps I should reconsider. I was accepted for a rotating or flexible internship at UAMSC in medicine.

After receiving my medical degree and license, I began to write prescriptions for various family members and friends, then keep a portion of each prescription for myself. Among doctors this is called "splitting scripts." I would also devour drug samples given or sent to me by drug company representatives; this is known as "eating your mail."

A few months after graduation, I figured I might as well go whole hog and reward myself in a major way. I wrote myself a large prescription for Demerol and shot it all that very night. I rationalized that I would do this only three or four times a year, so it wasn't a serious offense and I wouldn't get caught if I did it only rarely. Demerol, however, became increasingly difficult to obtain, mostly because my three or four times a year quickly became three or four times a month. I was very much afraid of being caught, despite my rationalizations, so I switched over to Mepergan (Demerol plus Phenergan), since it was only slightly less powerful than Demerol and easier to get.

Once I had successfully passed my first big prescription, I found it easier to rationalize passing others. For that first prescription, I had used my own name and gone to a drugstore in a distant neighborhood. Now I realized I could also pass prescriptions in other people's names—childhood friends, distant relatives, and anyone else I could think of. I had been a pro at passing forged scripts years before, and since I was now a licensed doctor, I felt justified. After all, my friends and relatives really did have migraine headaches, sciatica, and kidney stones; they "needed" medication. The fact that I always dipped generously into their supply or frequently passed prescriptions under other people's names (and took all the medication for myself) seemed only fair. My headaches, gastrointestinal difficulties, and joint pains "justified" my narcotic intake.

I had been using drugs for years, had survived, and had gotten away with it. I felt I deserved a reward. My knowledge regarding drugs was encyclopedic, but my denial was equally huge. I didn't consider my behavior abusive. After all, I prescribed for others. I saved lives. I made life-or-death decisions daily. Why shouldn't I prescribe for myself? Who was better qualified? Look what I had already experienced and lived through—must I not be invulnerable? I was in control. I was a hot-shot resident, here to save lives.

Now I had a virtually unlimited drug supply. What more could I ask for? I worked hard and I took hard drugs. I did both extremely well. I had made it. Nothing could stop me now.

Meanwhile, my self-esteem came to depend on how well I performed at work, which, in fact, was nothing new. It was crucial to my sense of well-being to be a good doctor. I attached myself fiercely to a rather interesting moral code: Never take drugs from patients and never have sex with a patient. This was drilled into us in medical school, and I became compulsive about it. I didn't violate this code, and I believed that if I could adhere to this specific code of ethics, then I had no problem. Deep down I knew what a horrible, sinful person I was because of my drug use, but no one else knew, and that was what mattered. At the same time, I needed constant encouragement; I had to be told how good I was, how much knowledge I had, how talented I was, and how many lives I saved.

In 1979 I won the Intern of the Year Award. I was then asked to speak to the incoming class of interns about what it meant to be a doctor, to accept responsibility, and to do good deeds. I gave my speech loaded on Valium, codeine, and scotch.

Dr. Warren has asked me to say a few words about this past year: These are the times that try men's and women's souls.

It seems like only yesterday I was sitting where you are now. I can't believe this year is over. My, how time flies when you're having fun!!!

This past year for me has been one of the best years of my life. It's also been one of the hardest and most stressful.

When I was going through orientation one year ago, I'll have to admit that I was pretty uptight. All of a sudden you're wearing a long white coat instead of a short one and a lot of people are asking you to make a lot of decisions—important decisions —and there won't always be someone there to help you with those decisions.

The difference between this coming year and the junior year (or the scut year as we know it) is the responsibility. As a junior, you were told what to do, where to do it, when to and how to do it. As an intern, you will also be telling others what to do and . . . the responsibility for the care of your patients will be on your shoulders!

There will be times when everyone will come down on you—doctors, nurses, lab (especially the lab), and even patients. If you're conscientious, there will be times that you will feel totally wasted . . . every fourth night call tends to do that to you. It will be depressing. When you take care of sick folks, some of them are going to die. And sometimes, no matter how hard we try, there is just not much we can do about it. We're not gods, although some of us like to think we are.

Nonetheless, what we all want to do is be a good doctor—the best—and there is only one way to do that: And that's to learn from every single experience that you have—whether it's good or bad.

What you need to do in order to keep your head

together this next year is to establish your priorities. First things first. What's important to you, what is best for the patient. The patient should always come first. But if you're not healthy, physically as well as emotionally, then you won't be able to do what's best for your patient.

Stay cool and keep smiling. A smile can be very good medicine. Stay flexible, friendly, cooperative, and considerate, and you should be able to run things smoothly.

For everything you put into this year, you'll get a whole lot more out of it. It's the year that can make you or break you.

Make the most of it! Be a good doc . . . and remember, do unto others as you would have them do unto you.

Have a good time!

Good luck!

To me, the content of this speech was ironic. Loaded on drugs at 8:00 A.M., I was telling other future physicians that docs aren't gods, that docs must take care of themselves physically and emotionally, and that docs must assume tremendous responsibility. Yet, I thought I was God, my physical and emotional state had already deteriorated significantly, and my drug-oriented activities were certainly irresponsible, at best. My level of denial was phenomenal. I couldn't see that the rules that applied to others also applied to me.

9

DR. ADDICT

You can't afford any less
  than perfection...
Otherwise—
  they lose faith
  and
You lose command!
MARTHA MORRISON, 1981

After I completed my internship in June 1979, I became a resident in psychiatry in the hospital where I had been treated just a few years earlier for drug abuse, depression, and schizophrenia. I had done it: I had graduated from medical school with honors, and now I was a resident, training in and practicing psychiatry just as Dr. Martin had done and just as I had vowed I would do nine years before.

Any psychiatric residency involves three years of specialized training in internal medicine and neurology, and on-the-job training in psychiatric services like consulting, teaching, and therapy. Ironically, part of my residency program involved teaching substance-abuse classes to medical students and consulting on drug-related cases in three different hospitals. I was assigned to most of the alcoholics and drug addicts who entered the state medical system because I was compassionate, determined, dedicated, and most of all, knowledgeable. Not surprisingly, I related well with the patients. Of course, I still honestly did not think that I was one of them.

I began my residency in July 1979, at the Child Study Center, working with mentally, emotionally, and behaviorally disturbed children and adolescents. This rapidly became my love and my specialized area of interest, probably because of my experience and hospitalizations as an adolescent, as well as my own immaturity.

Shortly after I began my residency, I became aware that I was having occasional blackouts. At this point, I had no idea that such memory losses were called blackouts or that a blackout was a symptom of severe addiction and of decreasing tolerance to drugs and alcohol. Occasionally I would also act disoriented and weird.

Invariably, these episodes occurred while I was high on narcotics. One evening at home, I became oddly disoriented and put a frozen dinner into the oven thinking it was the refrigerator. A few minutes later I began digging around in the freezer for my eyeglasses. Paul thought I was nuts. "What ever are you doing?" he said. I snapped back at him, as if nothing was odd: "I'm looking for my glasses! What did you think I was doing," and then I sort of laughed it off.

I quickly developed a reputation at work for being extremely obsessive-compulsive, and I was. In a sense, though, my compulsive habit of writing everything down had more to do with my subconscious realization that my memory functions were becoming impaired than with an innate obsessiveness—although I must admit, I am innately obsessive. For the first time, though, I realized I could not remember anything unless I wrote it down.

True to form, I also became compulsive about recording my drug use and drug-related activities. I began keeping track of the prescriptions I was writing for myself, for others, and for nonexistent persons; I recorded dates, quantities of drugs, and drugstores where the prescriptions had been filled. I wanted to be sure I did not write more than one prescription for the same person and have it filled at the same pharmacy in the same week. If a pharmacist became suspicious for any reason and decided to check his records, it would seem odd to him that a mere psychiatric resident was writing so many narcotic scripts. And God knows, I could not remember from one day to the next where I had passed a script.

For a period of time, I also kept the pill bottles and prescription labels as confirmation of the scripts I had passed. There is a real art, or a real insanity, to not getting caught passing bad scripts. And I never was.

In August 1979, Paul and I began to plan a trip to Europe, our second. I was looking forward to this trip. However, since we were planning to be out of the country for more than four weeks, I was worried about how I would replenish my drug supply while I was abroad. I would never approach anyone I did not know for drugs, particularly a stranger in a foreign country.

For days before we left, I carefully planned my anticipated use on a day-by-day basis. Alcohol was not a problem because I could buy it anywhere; I had cultivated a taste for warm 6 percent dark beer when we traveled in Europe a few years before. Pot, narcotics, speed, and tranquilizers were my main concerns because these drugs, in addition to alcohol, had become my mainstays. Therefore, I counted out and organized pills, calculating the bare minimum that I could get by with on any given day. I organized my marijuana supply, rolled joints, and planned how I would sneak them through customs. I hid some of the joints between two pairs of socks, which I always wore under hiking boots when we passed through customs, and I stuffed some of them inside my underwear.

We flew from Chicago to Luxembourg, and from there we went to Strasbourg, France, down the *rue de vin* to Basil and on to Bern, Switzerland. The *rue de vin,* or Wine Route, is every alcoholic's dream: miles and miles of vineyards with wine-tasting stands at very frequent intervals.

We traveled to Lauterbrunnen, Zermatt, and the Matterhorn in the Alps. These were the most impressive mountains that I had ever seen and the landscape was absolutely gorgeous. After climbing on the Matterhorn and hiking miles in beautiful pastel-flowered fields, we moved on to Italy and then traveled to Vienna. After Vienna, we proceeded to Innsbruck and then to Mieders, a small village in a valley, surrounded by phenomenal snow-capped mountains. We climbed Serles, a nearby peak, and I smoked a joint at the top to celebrate. In fact, I took drugs, smoked pot, and drank alcohol throughout the entire trip. But I controlled it—I had to because my supply was limited. We completed our trip by traveling through Bavaria, and I particularly enjoyed visiting King Ludwig's castles. I found this man morbidly fascinating and could relate to his power and madness.

I regret to say that I frequently behaved like a classic "ugly American" tourist. American grandiosity coupled with an addict's narcissism is of unparalleled obnoxiousness. I was utterly intolerant of others and their customs. Beautiful scenery and rich history whizzed by me, but I remained focused on my drug supply and the problems of transporting it between countries. Needless to say, I was very suspicious of the "foreigners." It never entered my mind that I was the odd one, the guest.

My husband knew I smoked pot and drank, but he was unaware of the extent of my use of other drugs. I know he had no idea I was carrying the speed or the narcotics. At times, it was tricky getting around him. Wide travel, varied cultural experiences, and close proximity with one's spouse always produce stress among addicts.

We returned to Arkansas in September, and I plunged right back into my residency in psychiatry and the merry-go-round of addiction. Professionally, I continued to perform well. I moved over to the state hospital to begin a six-month rotation with adult psychiatric inpatients.

I got to know Dr. Ralph Randall, one of my residency supervisors, during this rotation. He was a very knowledgeable, astute, and caring psychiatrist. I began giving grand rounds on drug abuse, drug overdoses, drug treatment. (Grand rounds are special presentations given to hospital staff, particularly those involved with a specific medical specialty.) I also continued teaching substance abuse and human sexuality courses to medical students. Toward the end of the year, I became involved with the medical school's admission committee and began interviewing medical school applicants. It seems ironic to me now that I was passing judgment on other people's qualifications to pursue a medical career.

The New Year, 1980, began with a trip to New Orleans with my brother and his family to attend the Sugar Bowl: Arkansas versus Alabama. The Razorbacks were soundly defeated which, of course, was a socially acceptable reason to tie one on down on Bourbon Street. I got drunk as a skunk, although I tried not to be too flamboyant because I didn't want to be a negative influence on my young nephews. I doubt that I succeeded, because I recall very little of that trip.

Ed Morrison: Late in her residency, probably about 1980, I noticed that Martha went from being overweight—puffy face, that sort of thing, to being very thin. As I've said, for a long time, we suspected she had a drinking problem. But I didn't see her that often, so it was very difficult to make a judgment.

Finally it was beginning to become apparent to me that drugs didn't make me feel good anymore. In the past, drugs and alcohol had always given me a high, made me feel good, allowed me to function. Despite plenty of evidence that drugs had made me physically and emotionally ill, I had failed to perceive the negative effects. My denial was in good order. But during my second year of residency, I was painfully aware that I was beginning to use drugs just to appear normal. I continued to function well. I was a workaholic, and I rarely missed work. When I did, it was virtually always due to a drug-related problem such as an overdose or septicemia.

As I became more knowledgeable about psychiatric disorders, I began to observe, and to fear, that I might be suffering from some of them myself. For example, I discovered that I exhibited symptoms of obsessive-compulsive personality disorder. I had researched and written an essay on the subject to share with the other residents. My "brief" explanatory presentation about this disorder ran over one hundred pages and probably could have sufficed for a doctoral thesis.

As I proceeded further into psychiatry—studying psychoanalytic history and theories, personality disorders, psychoses, neuroses, biological approaches, and treatment techniques—I began to learn much about myself. I became increasingly aware that I manifested the symptoms of certain psychiatric problems, and this made me even more paranoid. I looked everywhere for the good feelings drugs had once given me—work, family, sex, Razorback football games, horse races at Oaklawn, gambling, and parties—and I couldn't find them. I thought I was going crazy.

I decided to step up my drug intake. (Old habits die hard.) Throughout 1980, I ingested codeine and other synthetic narcotics, including Tylenol 3 and 4, Percodan, and Tylox, as well as tranquilizers, pot, and alcohol on a daily basis. To me, the hot-shot doctor, the narcotic or "downer" drugs seemed like the obvious solution to chronic stress. Moreover, I knew that stimulants—as much as I loved them—made me wired and paranoid, and so I avoided them, particularly speed and cocaine, at school or at work because I was afraid others would perceive that I was high. I figured I could hide behind tranquilizers or narcotics: Demerol and closely related drugs became favorites.

Although Demerol is a narcotic, a downer, it had a two-way effect on me—it both soothed me and perked me up. It allowed me to work longer hours, carry more patients, give more presentations, and take more weekend calls, yet at the same time, appear cool and calm. I still loved speed and cocaine, and always would, but for a while I used them less often.

I was also fast losing my tolerance for alcohol. I was getting drunk, a new experience for me, on two or three ounces of liquor, and invariably I would throw up blood after only a couple of drinks. In the past, I had been able to drink a fifth of whiskey and continue to function. I recognized that throwing up blood was not normal; this frightened me slightly, and I cut back on my drinking, but only slightly.

My physical deterioration was becoming as obvious as the decrease in my drug tolerance. My body was beginning to give out. By mid-1980, I had lost about 40 pounds, was throwing up blood frequently, had continual pain in my esophagus and stomach, which would become so sharp and penetrating during the night that it would wake me up. I was unable to eat, but I continued to drink and take dope, frequently tossing back the booze and pills with Maalox. At one point, I stopped drinking coffee for about six weeks in the hope that it would make me feel better.

Nevertheless, I never stopped taking codeine, Demerol, coke, and pot. I knew I had either an ulcer or acute gastritis, and so I prescribed Tagamet, an anti-ulcer drug, for myself.

Because Paul was very concerned about my health, I finally consented to see a physician. I went to my family doctor in Fayetteville, because, ironically, he was the only doctor I ever really trusted. He confirmed my diagnosis of acute gastritis and said to stay on the Tagamet, stop drinking alcohol and coffee, cut down on my smoking, stop working so damn hard, get some exercise, and eat frequent bland meals. (Of course, I didn't tell him about my drug intake.) I eventually got better, despite the fact that I continued to drink and take drugs.

In the summer of 1980, I attended my tenth high school reunion, and although I went to all the events, I recall very little. Several of my classmates congratulated me on my professional success, which was all I wanted; otherwise, all I remember was using tremendous quantities of alcohol, pot, and cocaine. Because I looked so thin and wasted, my old friend Joanie expressed great concern about my health. As she had done ten years before, she told me she was afraid I was killing myself. However, once again, I could not respond to her concern or her desire to help. I was too far gone.

During the fall of 1980, I began working with two people who became very close friends, Dr. Bill Davis and Maggie Peters, on a new Adolescent Inpatient Treatment Unit (AITU) at the state hospital. Bill, a psychiatrist, was the director of AITU, and Maggie was a psychiatric nurse who had special interest in adolescents.

I had heard about both Bill and Maggie before going over to AITU. Because both of them had strong personalities, most people figured we'd either all get along or we'd kill each other. The kids in the unit were also notoriously rough, and a story had circulated that one kid, who had been confined in seclusion, had kicked Bill in the groin. Before meeting Bill, I had begun to refer to him as Iron Balls Davis. On my first day in the unit, a guy walked up to me, stuck out his hand, and said, "Dr. Morrison? I'm Iron Balls Davis." For the first time in my life, I was absolutely speechless. I figured it took guts to make such a joke on himself, and that first meeting launched our friendship.

Maggie was equally witty and equally tough. She was a couple of years older than I, very attractive and energetic. Her husband, Mac, was a psychologist who worked with children in another part of the same medical complex. They lived in a big old rambling house and had two little kids. Maggie and I were extremely competitive with each other but in a friendly way, and as a result, we became very close friends very quickly.

We worked together intensively, scheming and planning for all sorts of programs and fighting for causes, like the right of adolescents to have individual treatment. The AITU grew despite resistance from the power source at the hospital who believed adolescents should be treated with adults, or not at all.

Maggie's and my personal friendship flourished, too. We would work intensely and then party intensely, often staying out until all hours drinking at local bars. Mac didn't seem to mind, and by this time, neither did Paul. But Maggie couldn't keep up with me. No one could. I was moving too fast.

Maggie Peters: We worked well together. We'd talk about doing a treatment program in Little Rock. Then we'd go to Fayetteville and decide that would be a great place for an adolescent unit. We had all kinds of ideas. We even thought about having a treatment program on a cruise ship. It's rare when you have the opportunity to work closely with a friend and share ideas about working together in the future. Most people can't work together and also be friends.

But I do think Martha's and my friendship was beginning to affect my marriage. Mac and Martha were also good friends— *are* good friends. I think they have their own special relationship. I'm not quite sure what that is, but that's fine with me. But, how many nights a week can you go out when you are a mother and a wife and come home at nine or ten on a school night feeling absolutely no pain?

At one point in time, Bill Davis told me he was concerned that I might be manic-depressive and encouraged me to get help. I now understand why he made that diagnosis. I cer-

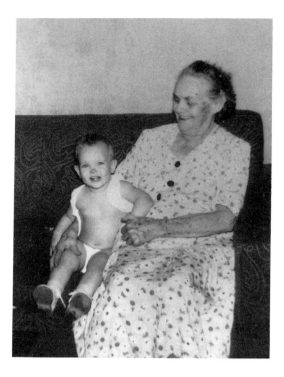

Mammy and me on my first birthday, July 1953.

Mamie Eisenhower, eat your heart out. My mother loved to dress me up. Apparently this outfit was a hit because this picture was used as an advertisement for Roy's Photo Shop in downtown Fayetteville in 1955.

"Reading" with my brother Eddie. Note my upside-down sensibility even at age three.

After a successful fishing
expedition with Daddy,
circa 1958.

Mother and Daddy with me, summer 1966.
This was about the time of the all-night
drinking spree following my fourteenth
birthday.

Christmas 1967, age fifteen.
Hair rollers indicate that
I had not yet gone
counterculture.

My high school graduation photograph, taken in September 1969, three months before my first hospitalization.

In my bedroom on "Falldown Street" with my dogs and my narcotics, winter 1972.

My aunt Tude receiving a service award for thirty-three years of work as a nurse. She was influential in my choice of a career in medicine. She also helped support me during college.

My graduation from med school, spring 1978.

With my mother, summer 1980, a year before the end.

Above:
Sober at last, November 1981.

Left:
Fishing in the Arkansas River close to the end, summer 1981.

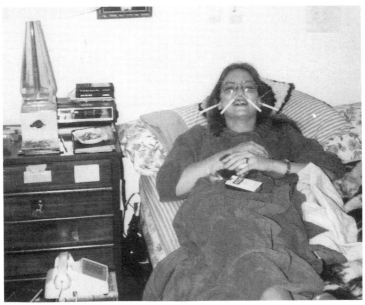

Sane, sober life in the halfway house, winter 1981–82.

At Calloway Gardens, the
annual Impaired
Professionals Retreat,
spring 1982. What? Me
impaired?

With Doug Talbott at the
World's Fair, Knoxville,
Tennessee, spring 1982.

Wedding, Talbott-style, with Polly, me,
Fog, Bob, and Doccy, Christmas Eve 1984.

Below:
Recent Razorback convert, Fog Talbott,
fall 1985.

Above:
Moments before the ceremony,
December 1984

Lecturing adolescents at
Ridgeview, spring 1984.

"The big one" and me, flanked
by my brother Ed and my
nephew, Key West, Florida,
October 1987.

tainly looked manic when I was using stimulants and depressed when I was using downers. It troubled me that he thought I was so ill. He encouraged me to seek private psychiatric help and to try lithium, but I didn't know how lithium would combine with the other drugs I was taking, so I hedged.

Maggie also knew I was frequently depressed and upset about my health. She often saw me acting crazy, but she also saw me perform exceptionally well. She became convinced that something was desperately wrong when I had a very noticeable blackout at work.

I was working on some charts at the Community Mental Health Center, and the next thing I remember I was standing in the parking lot talking with one of the hospital security men—four or five hours later. He told me that Maggie had tried to reach me; there had been an emergency. I had no idea what was going on and no memory of what I had been doing or where I'd been. I just woke up in the parking lot, talking to a cop. I told him I'd been in my office doing paperwork and hadn't heard any calls; I assured him that I would take care of the situation and thanked him. This blackout was more serious than any I had ever experienced, and it frightened me. What's more, Maggie was angry and concerned.

Maggie Peters: Martha and I called each other practically every night, and I knew she'd been depressed. One night I couldn't find her anywhere, and it sort of worried me. I figured she might be working late—at least, I hoped she was— so I called security at the hospital and had them go back and find out if her car was there. It was pretty late at night.

But I never thought anything was seriously wrong until one night a few months later we were sitting at the Tracks Inn, a local pub, and some pills fell out of my purse. Martha just scooped them up and drank them down with her scotch. I couldn't believe she was putting those things in her mouth.

They could have been cyanide pills, for all she knew.

Martha used to say, "Now, Maggie, trust me." And stupidly, I did, although we saw clues to her problems. For example, Mac once found a bunch of Southern Comfort bottles in her laundry basket. She told us she was collecting them to make candle lamps. She and I used to just drive around and talk sometimes—usually smoking dope the whole time—and I worried that the State Police would stop us. But I'd just put on my seat belt and trust her.

Connie Williams Kingston: During her marriage to Paul, Martha and I weren't as close as we'd been. I knew something wasn't right, but I didn't know what it was. We all thought she had anorexia. It was hard to reach her right then. She was good friends with Maggie at that time, and I felt like I'd lost her. I was real jealous of that relationship at first.

Martha would come over here in the afternoon or the early evening, maybe a couple of times a month. We went over to her house only a few times, but I wasn't sure what was going on day-to-day. I knew she used drugs, and I knew that the relationship with Paul wasn't what it should have been, but I always saw Martha when she was alone—not with him. She didn't talk about him that much; she never revealed anything intimate about herself.

I worked on the AITU for four months and then moved to the greater Little Rock Community Mental Health Center for another four months. I loved working with the adolescents. As a result, I pressed hard to get the psychiatry department at USMC to create a formal adolescent psychiatric fellowship that would allow one resident to specialize in this area. I, of course, would be the first recipient since I had firmly decided that adolescent psychiatry would be my specialty.

Toward the end of 1980, I had to decrease my intravenous narcotic use slightly because my tolerance had fallen dramatically and I could no longer function on the doses I was accustomed to injecting. Some people told me that I got violent on Demerol, which horrified me, but I didn't doubt it. I'm sort of a violent person—I like violent books, violent movies, firing an Uzi at a gun range. Once, during a blackout, I apparently beat up a friend of mine. When I came to, my other friends were amazed. They told me I'd been very aggressive. I didn't get the details because I quickly denied the whole thing to myself and just laughed it off and pretended I thought they were complete fools. They must have thought I was crazy.

I experienced blackouts every time I injected Demerol or Mepergan, and these episodes disturbed me greatly. To compensate, I began to increase my intravenous use of stimulants, particularly cocaine. I also continued to ingest orally Tenuate, Ritalin, Fastin, Valium, Ativan, Serax, Percodan, vitamins (ten or twelve a day), Cogentin, Artane, marijuana, alcohol, codeine, Tylox, and, when I could afford "controlled blackouts," Demerol or Mepergan.

In the spring of 1981, I overdosed badly on Mepergan (about 600 milligrams of meperidine, a narcotic, and 600 milligrams of Phenergan, a sedative). I had passed a prescription late in the afternoon and had decided to do only part of it—maybe five pills—and save the rest. I went home that evening and decided to shoot up in the bathroom. At this point, my marriage had disintegrated so badly that Paul and I were barely speaking. I had moved into our downstairs den and was sleeping on the sofa bed. One minute I was shooting dope in the bathroom, and the next thing I knew, I was coming to nine hours later in bed.

Paul told me later that he had found me in a semiconscious state lying on the bathroom floor in a pool of blood. I had a tourniquet around my thigh and was stabbing my leg with a syringe. Apparently, I had used all of the Mepergan—about thirty pills—in one or two hits. I recall none of this. The only drug I had ever injected intramuscularly—as opposed to intravenously—was heroin, never Mepergan or Demerol. Later he also told me that he had called Connie. She and her husband, Mike, had come over during the night to help me. They had attempted to reach a physician friend to get some Narcan, a narcotic antagonist used to reverse the effects of an overdose.

Connie Williams Kingston: Mike and I were in bed, sound asleep, and the phone rang. It was Paul. He said, "I think Martha's dead. Come quick!"—or something to that effect. Maybe he just said he couldn't wake her up. God, that was awful. I was terrified, but at the same time, I'd been through this sort of thing so many times with my brother, and I'd been worried about Martha so much, that I felt sort of fed up and angry. I do remember thinking, "Well, go ahead Martha. If you're going to die, then die."

We grabbed the baby—she was about three at the time—and Mike and I rushed over there. We walked in and saw Martha crumpled on the bathroom floor. She still had her tourniquet on and she was barely breathing. The needle was just lying there. I said, "My God, Paul, she needs to be in the hospital." But he said, "No, no, we can't do that." He had just left her there on the floor. I guess he couldn't lift her. Together he and Mike picked her up and put her on the bed.

Paul was having trouble handling this. Martha looked white around her mouth; as a matter of fact, she looked dead. I kept saying that we needed to take her to the emergency room, but Paul wouldn't hear of it. He kept saying, "No, it might ruin her career." So we hit her in the face and walked her around and around, and we finally put her to bed. She did make it known that she didn't want to be in the upstairs bedroom, but she never really woke up.

We talked all night. The three of us—Mike, Paul, and I—sat there on her bed and watched Martha and talked. Paul expressed a lot of concern for Martha. He said this couldn't go on, that she had to get help. After that, he would call me almost every day.

In fairness to Paul, I had told him a number of times in extremely strong terms that I didn't want to go to the hospital if I ever overdosed. I was dominating, hostile, threatening, and very insistent. I had said, "Don't you ever goddamn take me to the doctor or the emergency room if I overdose." That was my primary order—one of the few direct and uncompromising orders I ever gave him.

I recovered, but nothing felt very good after that. I worked longer and longer hours, increasing my sixteen-hour-a-day work load to compensate for the fact that everything in my life—my health, my marriage, my work, my well-being—had gone to hell. I became increasingly depressed and lost still more weight. The memory losses became more frequent and serious. I stopped communicating with my parents and my brother. My husband and I had terrible fights. During one battle I knocked a large hole in our bedroom wall and then didn't even remember doing it. I seriously considered suicide and began to carry a prescription for Dilaudid and a syringe in my purse at all times so I could kill myself on the spot if my pain became absolutely unbearable. I had lost control of my life; the least I could do was maintain control over my death.

I became even more convinced that I was suffering from a major psychiatric disorder, but I had been using drugs for years, so I figured that my craziness couldn't be related to the drugs. For five days in March 1981, I stopped using all drugs except one joint at night. As a result, I became catatonic, paranoid, and psychotic. That clinched it. I was certain that I was either schizophrenic or manic-depressive and that I was using drugs to cover up my illness. It never occurred to me that I was experiencing withdrawal. In fact, I reasoned that I should start the drugs all up again and use more of them so I wouldn't appear quite so crazy.

Here was the superstar doctor, the prize-winning resident, unable to diagnose classic drug-withdrawal symptoms. And my symptoms were blatant: I was hyperactive to the point of mania; I slept less than three hours a night; I had lost masses of weight and was probably anorexic; I was experiencing overwhelming depression; I was frequently confused, disorganized, disoriented, and unable to remember things or to concentrate; and I sometimes experienced psychomotor retardation. I felt suicidal, and profoundly hopeless, helpless, and worthless. I might have gotten help if it had not been for the guilt. My guilt, at this time, had become absolutely overwhelming.

I ruminated obsessively about all the horrible things I'd done. I became convinced that I was killing my patients. However, I continued to receive reassurance from the staff that I was "the best." This, too, was confusing because I felt like I was in hell. And I was.

I turned again and again to the only thing that had ever worked for me, the only thing I cared about, the only thing I trusted—the drugs—but they no longer worked for me. I was using twelve different drugs on a daily basis, including alcohol. I was consuming such quantities of drugs that even I— who had years of street connections, physician connections, drug company representative connections; who grew my own, wrote my own, and had at times manufactured my own—could no longer keep myself in supply. I could not get enough to make me feel good. I was just barely able to reach the point where I acted and felt normal, and normal, for me, was no longer very good. I wrote more and more prescriptions; I knew I'd be dead long before my narcotics license was endangered.

Finally I focused on cocaine, the king. Nothing compared to the high from this drug, and nothing compared to my compulsive, irrational need for this drug. I began injecting a gram of pure USP cocaine—a huge amount—into my veins in a single hit, using one-half to one ounce a day. I was blowing my head off, developing myoclonic (seizure-like) activity, and experiencing incredible cardiac arrhythmias (irregular heartbeat). But the high would last only a few seconds, and then I was miserable again. Nothing worked.

I went to Dr. Randall, with whom I had developed a fairly close relationship, and said that I wanted to quit my residency, that I was not cut out to be a physician or a psychiatrist. He said he thought I was just tired, depressed, and overworked, and suggested that I try psychotherapy. He referred me to one of the most highly regarded private psychiatrists in the state, Dr. Carter, who had been a resident at the med school several years before.

I was depressed and overworked, but I was also in the terminal stages of my addiction and couldn't tell anyone, mostly because I didn't know it. Therefore, I lied and denied and presented a very confusing clinical history to my psychotherapist. I did finally tell Dr. Carter that I was taking heavy doses of drugs, however. He diagnosed me as "a substance abuser with reactive depression and obsessive-compulsive personality disorder," and he prescribed large doses of Sinequan, an antidepressant.

I began to eat better and was able to continue working. Nothing else changed. I quickly regained fifteen pounds, which alarmed me because I thought my "model-like" thinness was attractive. What's more, it calmed me to believe I had "control" over my weight. I stopped the Sinequan and became truly anorexic. I would eat just enough to force people to stop bugging me about my weight; however, I became compulsively organized about my food. I would eat things in threes or fives—three kernels of corn or five green beans, depending on whether I reasoned that I deserved more food or less. Twenty minutes after a meal I would make myself throw up, reasoning that I had allowed my body enough time to absorb a few nutrients but not to gain weight. I believed that my weight and my death were the only remaining aspects of my life over which I had control.

Through psychotherapy, Dr. Carter helped me gain insight into some of my problems and my personality, but not my addiction. He helped me to see that, drugs or no drugs, I was angry, immature, impulsive, insecure, terrified, constantly punishing myself, caught in a profession that was tearing me apart despite the fact that I was good at it, and caught in a marriage that had been pathological from the beginning. The insights were astonishing to me, and the more self-perception I gained, the more drugs I took.

Dr. Carter recommended hospitalization several times because I was so depressed and suicidal. I'd be manic for days, then catatonically depressed for even longer. He, too, began to think that I was manic-depressive when in reality I was hyperactive and paranoid from the cocaine and other stimulants, and depressed and sluggish from the narcotics. Because my behavior at home was so erratic, my husband was equally concerned and also wanted to have me hospitalized.

I couldn't let them hospitalize me. I knew what psychiatric hospitals were like. I was the local expert, and I knew that the treatment available did not hold the answers for me. It is very difficult for a doctor to hospitalize a hot-shot colleague with an excellent reputation. It's even more difficult for a husband to commit a wife, especially one who is a psychiatrist. And so I became more and more firmly trapped. The ring of pain tightened. I did the only thing I knew how to do: I used more drugs and more alcohol.

In June 1981, I was offered the chief residency, but I refused the appointment. I could not handle any more responsibility. I had now completed my third year of postgraduate training and was entering my fourth and final year. I continued teaching, giving lectures and presentations, carrying patients, taking calls, and serving on the admissions committee. I had built

an outstanding reputation for myself, but all of the glory—
together with my pride and denial—prevented my salvation.

I couldn't get high and I couldn't come down. I was
caught—desperate and doomed. I was sick and tired of being
sick and tired. I was without hope. And I knew I was dying.

10
APOCALYPSE NOW

This is the end, one way or the other—
professionally, personally, and socially.
This is the end.
This is finally the end of it all.
I must die!
It is the only end—now.
MARTHA MORRISON, 1981

The last few months before I entered treatment were probably the worst months of my life. Although I didn't know it then, and did not fully understand it until long after I entered treatment, I was at the phase that professionals call "end stage addiction"—in other words, I was very close to death. With the knowledge that I could obtain a large dose of Dilaudid at anytime, I was operating under the assumption that I had my death under control. But, in fact, my death was probably far more imminent than I realized. Writing in my diary became one of the few things that held me together. Some of the passages I wrote during those last weeks reveal not only my craziness but also my suicidal tendencies.

June 1, 1980
I know I will die soon. I have almost come to reckon with that. I've been driven to this since I was born. Mammy died when I was five. It was years before I realized I could not possibly have under-

stood the meaning of death at that age. I still don't.

I watch my lonely life unfold. I see it every day. I can't live with the contradictions. I must break on through. The road is narrow, but I will pass. There is time, although not much.

My mother demanded perfection, and she got it but not without extreme limit-testing. Daddy was passive, but I love him more than anyone. At seventeen they committed me to a mental hospital. Ah, the beginning and the end. I knew then that the end would come ten years later. I bought a year somehow. I have known all along; I just never knew exactly when. Now I know.

I always went to church. Baptist—what else?— every Sunday morning, afternoon, and evening. I went every Wednesday evening. I went to every fellowship, revival, and study course. I was district champion in the four-state Bible drill contest. Not only can I name all the books of the Bible in one breath, but I can spell them, too. The churchgoing finally went by the wayside when I was seventeen.

Since then, it's just been dope—little else.

No one gets out of here alive.

No one here gets out alive.

June 3, 1981

I have just met with Dr. Randall, and I told him most of what I've been trying to tell Dr. Carter for five weeks. It is my decision to terminate therapy. My bills to him are paid, but I deserve the privilege of going in one more time and telling him what a jerk I think he is. I'm so furious at everybody and everything.

For the last five sessions, I have gone in there determined to tell Carter that I can't talk to him, that he pisses me off, that I don't trust him, and that I don't think we're getting anywhere in therapy. But I can't do it.

I am killing myself, the deadline is July 1—or maybe July 10—how appropriate, my twenty-ninth birthday. I can't even make it till I'm thirty.

I've lived more, loved more, lost more, found more, and dreamed more than most do in a lifetime. And for that I'm grateful.

How naive. I have not really been in touch with my feelings for years. When is the last time I felt and recognized anxiety? So long I can't remember. What have I done with it? Kept it under control? Usually my obsessiveness and compulsiveness help me function well and suppress anxiety, but when they begin to surface, what do I do so often? Smoke, drink, and take codeine. No wonder I've not been able to recognize my anxiety. So I cut it off, along with my anger. So controlled, so over-controlled. What a facade. A wall, the Great Wall of China. I've got some sociopathy, but not much. My superego sees to that.

God, I'm so guilty.

I lie, rarely.

I skip Monday afternoon conferences.

I've written prescriptions for others and used the medication.

I shoot cocaine.

I shoot Demerol.

I'd shoot heroin and crystal if I had it.

I've hurt people.

I'm impulsive and will take most risks—lately all risks.

I smoke a tremendous amount of pot and consume massive quantities of alcohol.

I want power, but . . . I'll never deserve it.

I have a bad Electra complex.
I'd like to blow something up . . . myself.

Although many of my relationships were quickly breaking down—most stunningly my relationship with Paul—my friendship with Maggie was flourishing and becoming increasingly symbiotic. We were together from morning to night—working hard during the day and then playing with equal, and crazy, intensity at night. Every evening we'd go to the Tracks Inn or Bennigan's, two local joints that catered to younger professionals, and I would drink myself into oblivion. Occasionally we'd pick up guys—usually guys eight or ten years younger than we were—just to see if we still had our charms. Nothing serious ever developed. We'd have a few drinks and behave like a couple of rebellious teenagers.

Because Maggie was so game for acting crazy, I was able to get from our wild adventures some of the intensity I could no longer get from drugs. At work, we'd rush around all day, dealing with patients, making bizarre plans for new treatment facilities, and flirting with our colleagues. (We had a particular "thing" with one doctor. We dubbed him E.G.D.—Every Girl's Dream—and sent him gushy cards on Valentine's Day. He loved the attention.) At night, we'd head out to the Tracks, get drunk, get high—get off. Then I'd go home, try to sleep, get up at six, put out the dogs, drive to work, and start the mad routine all over again. It all gave me sort of a rush, and I depended on Maggie to provide the company.

By June 1981, my marriage had disintegrated totally. Since I had moved from our bedroom to our downstairs den months before, we were living as though we were separated. Finally, even that arrangement became untenable, and I began staying many nights at Maggie and Mac's house.

In late June 1981, I decided to take a couple of weeks off to rest. For days on end, I sat in our house, often on the bottom step, just staring into space, depressed as hell. Maggie would telephone me every day, and I know she became more and more alarmed at the severity of my despondency.

Maggie Peters: Martha was really stressed out during the spring and summer of 1981. At one point, she took several days off work, but she didn't seem to rally. I got so frightened that I came by and brought a pizza and a Mickey Mouse storybook and read to her for an hour. I knew her marriage was really bad, but I didn't really comprehend at that time the extent of her problems.

Even now I find it almost impossible to describe my hopelessness at this time. Most of my relationships were in shambles. I was barely keeping up with most of my friends and my family. My marriage was virtually over, and I felt guilty about that, knowing that I had not been what you'd call an ideal wife. Physically, I was wasted. All my life, I'd possessed what seemed like boundless energy, but now I felt exhausted all the time and was unable to accomplish anything. I was screwing up at work—forgetting meetings, becoming impatient and hopeless about patients. But worst of all, I just didn't care. The uppers or downers, once my life's blood, did nothing for me. But of course, never once did it occur to me that drugs might, in fact, be my problem. I felt tired and guilty. So very, very guilty.

After my two-week respite, I decided I had no choice but to quit my residency. I felt that I had lost my sensitivity, intuition, and feeling. I was missing work consistently and believed that I was irresponsible and had no business trying to care for patients. I couldn't be depended on to do anything. Finally, I spoke to Dr. Randall about this, but he refused to let me quit. So I kept on living my one-day-at-a-time existence, unsure where to turn or what to do.

In mid-July, Paul and I began to talk seriously about divorce, although by that time I was in no condition to discuss anything "seriously." I did decide to move in with Maggie and her family more or less permanently, though, and that move made our separation formal. I stayed with the Peters family for about a month, then returned home while Paul went on a three-week trekking vacation out west.

Maggie Peters: When Martha was living with us, she was like one of the household. There is no such thing as a guest in our house. You are either part of this family or you don't live here. Martha was part of the family. She'd pick up the kids after school and go to the lake with us every weekend. She was like a sister to me, even if we were real crazy at the time.

By early August 1981, I had begun to have blackouts of a duration and intensity that I found utterly terrifying. I bought some high-grade Tibetan opium from one of my connections and shot about 50 milligrams one night. I nodded off, but got up the next morning and went to work. I managed to function all day, but I was somewhat spaced out and I left early. At this time, I was living in my own house while Paul was away.

I started to drive home, but when I got about three miles from our house, I lost consciousness briefly and ran off the road, barely missing a row of mailboxes. I pulled the car back onto the road, drove along for another couple of miles, blacked out again, and smashed into a parked car, doing over $2,500 worth of damage to it and to my own car.

This experience appalled me, not only because of the damage I'd done, but because I realized that I might easily have killed a child, a jogger, or some other innocent. This scared the holy shit out of me and increased my already tremendous guilt.

On August 12, 1981, I received a very mysterious and disturbing phone call at work, from two doctors who claimed they were from an organization called the Arkansas Impaired Physicians Committee. They told me their names were Harvey

Irwin and Ron Brooks, and said they had to meet with me that night—it was urgent. I invited them to meet me at the hospital or my office, but they insisted that their information was personal as well as professional. I finally consented to meet them at my home at about nine, after I had finished work. I thought the late hour would put them off, but they agreed to meet me then.

As soon as I hung up the phone, I went into a panic. Who were these guys? Mafia? Narcs? Was I in trouble for passing scripts? I immediately phoned Maggie and told her what had happened. Because I always responded to everything with "junkie paranoia," it never even crossed my mind to confide in anyone other than Mag. I didn't leave work that evening until close to ten—again hoping they'd give up and leave. Right before I left the hospital, I called Maggie and instructed her to call the police if I did not phone her again within an hour.

I went flying down the street in front of my house, smoking a joint, thinking—hoping—they would be long gone. But when I turned the corner onto my street, which was a cul-de-sac, I saw what looked like a dozen cars, lights glaring, all parked in front of my house. One was a police car with a swirling blue light; another was a large white car with two or three people in it. The street looked like a carnival at high noon. I thought seriously about turning around, hauling ass, and driving to Mexico. I knew I had been busted. There was dope all over the house, and hundreds of marijuana plants were growing in my garden. It was finally all over, I thought. It was finally over.

But I could run no longer. I pulled into my driveway and prepared for the worst. With the last bit of arrogance I could muster, I got out of the car and said in my most polite Baptist-Sunday-school voice, "What seems to be the matter, Officer?"

One of the cops told me he was a friend of Maggie's. She had called him and reported that several suspicious individuals were waiting at my house. But the cop said that he had questioned them and learned that they were both physicians. They wanted to talk to me about something professional.

My neighbors were peering from their windows and standing on their front steps, which embarrassed me, but I preferred to be red-faced in front of my neighbors rather than let cops into my house. Moreover, I would rather have been attacked by Godzilla than busted. I assured the cops that I recognized these people, that everything was okay, that Maggie was overly concerned. I thanked them—still politely—and sent them on their way. Then I invited the strangers into my house.

Maggie Peters: I remember when those hit men showed up at Martha's house. She didn't know who they were; all she knew was that they were going to show up at her house in a white Cadillac. There would be either two or three of them.

It sounded really suspicious, so I called this friend of mine who is an undercover detective for the LRPD and asked if he could have a police car come to Martha's house. He said, "Shouldn't we go inside?" When I said no, he said, "Why not? You mean if we go in, we'll find something we don't want to find?" And I said, "Probably, Joe." So Joe sent a police car to Martha's house.

She called me after they left and told me that they were from the Impaired Physicians Committee and they suspected that she was an addict.

When they told me they were from some sort of society for impaired physicians, I thought, "How nice—blind, crippled, paralyzed docs." Then they detonated the bomb: They told me they knew I had a severe alcohol and drug problem. They were here to help me, not to hurt me or turn me in. Ron

Brooks told me he had had a problem primarily with alcohol. Harvey Irwin said he'd been busted for drugs and alcohol and had even had his license revoked for two years. Both claimed they were active in Alcoholics Anonymous, and Harvey said he had been through a treatment program.

They listed everything I was taking, including the opium, which astonished me, because I thought my dealer was the only person who knew I had opium. I truly believed that no one knew how many drugs I had been taking, but somehow these two men had put all the pieces together. They knew I had lost over forty pounds, that I was having difficulty at work, that I had marital problems, and that I was in psychotherapy.

Then they really laid it on. They said they knew I had been writing prescriptions for myself and splitting prescriptions with other people. They told me it was only a matter of time before the State Board of Medical Examiners got me. The Arkansas board was very strict about drug regulations; if Ron and Harvey had this information, others did, too.

Although I didn't recognize their compassion at the time, I realize now that they were incredibly sensitive. They said they understood what it was like to be afraid every time the phone rang or every time there was a knock on the door. They tried to tell me what a relief it would be to admit that alcohol and drugs were my problem—not mental illness, not insanity, not depression. They tried to tell me that I didn't have to do it alone.

I had sat and listened, drinking a scotch and water. I denied everything and told them indignantly that I didn't do drugs and had never written any prescriptions I did not feel were justified or medically indicated. I denied any type of alcohol or drug problem and admitted only that I'd had a problem as an adolescent, which was a matter of public record.

They questioned me as to whether I had examined every patient I had written prescriptions for and whether I had kept medical records. "Well, not all," I admitted. They informed me that writing unrecorded prescriptions was a violation of the Harrison Narcotic Act, punishable by fine and imprisonment.

Finally, they told me about a four-month program at Ridgeview Institute in Atlanta for doctors with drug problems. The treatment program had been designed by G. Douglas Talbott, a doctor who was highly respected for his work with impaired physicians. They explained that doctors from all over the United States and Canada had received help through this program, which was recognized and approved by the A.M.A. and the Arkansas State Medical Board. If I didn't want to go to Atlanta, I could go to a similar program in Jackson, Mississippi, which had been set up by one of Talbott's protégés. They insisted that I needed to enroll in one of these programs before I lost my medical license.

I could not believe this was happening to me. I just sat there dumbfounded. The last grains of my sanity slid through the hourglass. I numbly recall that they went on and on about AA, group therapy, and other doctors with drug problems. They told me I was going to keep hurting unless I took action. They told me I was dying and, in fact, had no alternative but to seek help.

Yet I insisted that I was no longer abusing drugs. I told them I had become depressed because of my marital problems; I was overworked; I was trying to put my life back in order with psychiatric help. I assured them that I was feeling much better. They just hugged me. I thanked them for their concern and apologized for having kept them waiting. And then I showed them out.

Ron Brooks: At the time of our intervention on Martha, I was living down in Pine Bluff, Arkansas, and had become friendly with Brad Williams. Brad and his sister, Connie, approached me because they knew I had an interest in intervention. At that time, Brad had been a friend of mine for several months. He told me that he was upset about his ex-wife. His sister had told him that Martha was in trouble with drugs and alcohol.

They gave me her husband's number, and I talked to Paul a couple of times. He was a real rigid type, very concrete, black and white, no gray. He had no idea what to do about Martha's problem, and he was scared. He wanted her to quit taking drugs, but he was heavily co-dependent. Co-dependents think that if their addict can stop drinking or taking drugs, everything will be wonderful. Then they realize that when their loved one gets sober, things will change completely and they will lose control.

Yet, when I called him, he was willing to let me try to do something for Martha. He told me he would be away for a couple of weeks; he said he had to be out of the house when we intervened, because Martha wouldn't even talk with us if she thought he had anything to do with the intervention.

I had met Harvey Irwin at some meetings, and he had introduced me to the idea of intervention. Martha was our first time out—our first intervention. We moved on her within two or three days of my first conversation with Brad. We felt like a couple of criminals.

Before intervening, Harvey and I talked to Brad, who had gotten most of his information from Connie, and of course we also spoke with Paul. Through them, we knew Martha was splitting scripts, shooting up, and taking every sort of drug—uppers, downers, sidewinders. Each one knew about particular drugs and her history with them, so we put their information together. One of them told us she was taking a lot of codeine—"eating her mail," as we say. She was also going to work screwed up. Somebody told us that she had lost a lot of weight recently, too. We called Martha at work. I remember she was the admitting physician that day. We told her we were from the Impaired Physicians Committee. As a matter of fact, there was no such group at that time in Arkansas—we just made it up. There were such boards in Louisiana and Texas, but nothing like that in Arkansas, so we were careful not to imply that we were in any way associated with the Arkansas State Medical Board.

We told her we'd meet her at her house that evening. We knew Paul wouldn't be there—he'd gone hiking or something—but he had given us the address. So Irwin and his wife and I drove over in his big white Cadillac. God, we were nervous that night. Martha wasn't home when we got there, so we sat in the car and waited. I guess the neighbors got worried, because the police came by and asked us what we were doing. We said we were Dr. Brooks and Dr. Irwin and we were waiting for Dr. Morrison. They bought that—as soon as you say you're a doctor, people think you're God. We waited for a long time—several hours—but we figured she had to come home sometime.

Martha finally drove up, and she was real shook, like a wild malnourished deer. Irwin flashed this phony card at her—like he was Jack Webb or something, and she asked us to come inside.

She looked like an inmate of Auschwitz or Buchenwald, but her eyes weren't glazed over, just terrified. She was experiencing such gross tremors that she could barely light her cigarette, and then she couldn't get it to her mouth. She just sat there shaking, with her arms wrapped across her chest, giving off a negative message in body language. Her health had obviously deteriorated, and we knew that her drug taking was interfering with her work. It is classic with addiction that once it starts to intrude in your work, you're at the end, and she was clearly at end stage addiction.

But she didn't make us leave. I guess she was scared. She didn't know who we were, so she figured she'd better go along with us. But she denied everything. She said she didn't use any drugs, that she occasionally drank a little vodka—that was it.

We told her about treatment. We knew about Doug Talbott in Atlanta and Doyle Smith in Jackson. We told her she had to call us the next day, and we said she had two options—she could go to Georgia or she could go to Mississippi.

Brad Williams: The only significant connection that I had with Martha after our divorce was with her intervention. Actually, I wasn't responsible for Martha going into treatment; I was just a messenger. Connie was worried about Martha. Every once in a while she would say, "Martha's having all these problems. Is there anything you can do?" I was living in Pine Bluff—Pine Bluff is forty miles from and a hundred years behind Little Rock—where I was director of a rehab program. I had a friend down there, Ron Brooks, a physician who was interested in intervention.

It was real funny timing. Ron had told me about this guy, Harvey Irwin, who was working with addicted physicians. Ron said, "I think it's going to be neat trying to work with other physicians." He had this new approach—doing interventions on doctors. Connie had just asked me if there was anything I could do to help Martha, so I gave Martha's name to Ron and told him I didn't know what kind of response he'd get, but good luck.

Ron told me what happened, and Connie later told me that Martha had gone to Atlanta. That was all I had to do with it—I just passed her name along.

Connie Williams Kingston: I did not talk to Ron Brooks directly, but I served as the go-between for Brad and Paul. They couldn't even be civil to each other. I started talking to Brad occasionally about Martha's problems. By this time Brad had been in AA for quite a while. At first he said, "Martha's going to have to get help on her own. There's nothing anybody can do for her." But I kept bringing it up, and evidently I said it enough times. Finally he said to me, "I think I know somebody who might be able to help her." I gave Paul the information, and he got in touch with Ron, I guess.

Paul had been calling me ever since the night of Martha's big overdose a couple of months before, but I didn't know what to do to help her. I thought it was interesting that Paul would be so open. He would talk and talk. I felt responsible; I thought Paul was asking me for help and that it was up to me to get it.

This was the summer of 1981. I remember thinking that something was about to happen. I just knew either she was going to leave Paul or she was going to die. It was fifty-fifty.

I had lived through this since high school with my brother; there were times when I wished he would just go ahead and die and get it over with. I was tired of this. And I was starting to feel that way about Martha that summer. She was real sick, and it was either time for her to die or time for her to get well.

Paul told me that the intervention was going to take place while he was away on vacation. Martha was not supposed to have any support; she had to be confronted on her own. I know Paul wanted Martha to go to Atlanta, but I think he would have liked to control the situation more. He knew what the alternatives were—and they were in Atlanta.

After Harvey and Ron left, I really lost it. I started drinking straight scotch and smoking dope. Actually, I got really lit. I knew my time was up. I probably thought about leaving the country, but I suspect my decision to not leave was made that night when I didn't run when I saw the flashing blue light on that cop's car.

For seventeen years I'd been doing this and I had no energy left. I hadn't been able to get off on dope for a long time. My whole life had gone to shit. My medical practice was the only thing I had left, and I was losing my ability to function as a doctor. I couldn't leave town, yet I couldn't work. If I went to Atlanta, I knew I'd get busted, and if I stayed in Arkansas, I knew I'd die. All the years of cons, scams, and games had come to an end. Nothing was left.

I was astonished that Ron and Harvey knew so much about me, but despite the extent of their knowledge, they had left out plenty. Although I denied my addiction to Ron and Harvey, and to myself, a secret part of me knew I couldn't live without drugs. I remember telling them, at one point of suppressed hysteria, that I didn't give a shit if I lost my license. I believed it was a moot point; I was going to die anyway—drugs or no drugs.

I called Maggie Peters and Joe Brady, my old rehab counselor, with whom I'd maintained a close friendship. I told them what had happened. Although I didn't tell them that the only way out that I could see was suicide, I let on that I suspected these men were on to something. They both told me that they loved me, that I probably had an alcohol and drug problem, and that I should probably do what Harvey and Ron recommended. They told me they would help me any way they could.

When I woke up the next morning I realized that I had not cared about my job, my medical license, or anything else for a long time. I had become a vacuum. I was barely existing. I could not eat or sleep. I was down to 111 pounds. I was exhausted. So I did the only thing I knew how to do: I took drugs and I went to work.

I took notes over the next few days, which I spent alone in Paul's and my house when I wasn't at work.

August 13: Losing it bad. Crying. More and more behind, as usual. Worked from 7:00 A.M. to 8:30 P.M.

Really exhausted but somewhat relieved. Drank sixteen cups of coffee and ate four aspirin. Feel like strangling Paul.

August 14, Friday: Cry. Fished at river. Beer/food/barf. Smoked opium.

August 15, Saturday: Fished from 7:00 A.M. to 7:00 P.M. Opium. Cry.

August 16, Sunday: Twelve hours' sleep. Bad cry. Cleaned garage. Did three loads of wash. Sprayed dogs for fleas. Dusted house. Ironed. Dictated for six hours. Ruminated for four hours. Cleaned and vacuumed and dusted for two hours (absurd). Cleaned bathroom for three hours (really absurd). Deny, deny, deny. Called my brother. Must tell parents. Baby, have you got it in you?

August 17, Monday: Will talk to Carter, Harvey, Ron, Brady, Maggie. I guess I've known I needed to go. I do have a very significant drug problem. I must resolve it now if I want to continue in my profession. Or must I? The only other alternative is death. I must resolve it now or else I will commit suicide—on purpose or via an accidental OD. Can I overcome this problem? I never have before.

But I've never been in this situation before either.

The initial relief I felt when those guys left was unmistakable, then and now. God, I spent seventeen years of my life trying to convince people I'm not a drug addict, only to find out that I am. But I've been through all this before. Then go through it again, dummy. Maybe you'll learn.

Can I face this again?

I gamble with the biggies only when I know I have a damn good chance of winning—that means go away.

*Otherwise get out now. You'll never be what you
want to if you don't face it now.*

*I love you all. Forgive me. Daddy, Eddie, Tray,
Mother, Brady, Connie, Paul, Dr. Randall, Maggie.
Even you, Carter.*

*I've just got to get away—professionally, person-
ally, interpersonally, therapeutically. I've got to look
at it from a distance. And at what has always been
the most significant thing in my life—drugs. Thank
you, everyone who has stuck through this with me.
You know who you are. Suicide is selfish, remember
that.*

Keep on trying, truckin'. Hang in there.

I am stuck at seventeen, unable to grow.

Maggie Peters: I remember driving around with Martha
after the intervention, and Martha saying, "How does anyone
know I've been splitting scripts?"

I knew what we'd been doing, and it was no big deal. We'd
been going out after work, smoking a couple of joints, going to
the Tracks Inn, and drinking margaritas until late hours. I
didn't know that she was doing anything in addition to that.
To me, it was no big deal. I knew other physicians who were
drinking and smoking pot, and they were not approached by
men in white Cadillacs. Drinking and smoking were not that
serious.

She was very paranoid. She wouldn't go to Atlanta. She said
she didn't need to go. She said, "If I have to go, I'll go for a
short period of time." In between, she was talking about going
to Mexico. And I thought all we were doing was smoking a
couple of joints. The penalty didn't fit the crime.

I met with Harvey and Ron a second time on Monday,
August 17. I made them meet me at Bennigan's so I could
drink. I admitted to a small problem shooting dope, but stated

absolutely that I had no intention of quitting pot or alcohol. At the same time, I asked them many questions about treatment. Despite my experiences ten years before with drug treatment and my two years of psychiatric residency that focused on drug abuse, I had never heard of this form of treatment. In a certain way, this moment marked the zenith of my denial. I coped beautifully when treating other drug addicts, but could not even comprehend dealing with my own addiction. I don't think I would have gone to meet them if I hadn't pretty much made up my mind to go into treatment. At the same time, I thought of it as a kind of death. I figured I could kill myself in Georgia more easily than I could in Arkansas.

They strongly recommended the Atlanta program because they felt that the only person who could really help me was this guy, Doug Talbott. I had to wait two weeks to get a bed, but I took their advice and made arrangements to go to Ridgeview.

Ron Brooks: I called her back—I really can't remember when. Harvey and I met her at Bennigan's, I guess. She kept asking where we'd got all this stuff on her. I also remember that she had a couple of drinks. But I got the impression that she was going to go to Ridgeview. She didn't tell us that she had gone, but we heard later that she'd gone down to Atlanta.

Connie Williams Kingston: Martha came and told me [about the intervention]. My face went red because I knew I'd been part of it. I was not going to tell her, and she didn't ask me. She was just appalled that anyone would do this to her. At first, she didn't say that she would go, but I could hear in her voice that she was ready.

On August 21, I went to Fayetteville and told my parents that some people thought I had a drug problem and had recommended that I go into treatment and I guessed I was going. They were very supportive and even seemed relieved. I think they were afraid I was going to die soon. While I was in Fayetteville I injected one ounce of USP coke over a period of three days, using one gram per injection. I figured I'd just blow it out.

Doyle Morrison: We really thought she'd quit taking drugs quite some time ago, but evidently she hadn't. She drank quite a bit. We worried more about the drinking than about the drugs. I'm sure we mentioned it to her a few times. She could hold quite a bit. After she married Paul, she bought whiskey by the case—she always had money.

Right before she went to Atlanta, we saw that she was depressed quite a lot. She and I went fishing up on the lake and talked about it—about her having trouble and having to do something. She had all her plans made. She felt she should do what the doctors had advised her to do. She didn't give us many details—just that she was going to Atlanta. We were relieved that she was going. We had no idea what was ahead of her. We were glad because we felt she needed help.

When Paul returned from his vacation, I moved back with Maggie and her family until it was time to go to Atlanta. For a while, I continued to use tremendous quantities of drugs, both overtly and secretly. I got the feeling that Maggie was relieved I was going into treatment. I know she was afraid my death was imminent.

As my departure time grew near, I tried to cut down. Most people blow it out before they begin treatment, and I had indulged this impulse to some extent during my visit with my parents. But part of me—the denial part of me, the perfectionistic, guilt-ridden part of me—thought that if I didn't cut down, they wouldn't let me in. I still took Percodan and codeine to keep me going, and of course I smoked pot and drank, but I tried to cut down.

Finally, I spoke to Dr. Randall and Dr. Carter and told them I was going for treatment. Dr. Randall was shocked to hear that I had a serious drug problem. At the same time, he was supportive of my going for treatment—at least at first. Later, he seemed upset when my hospitalization was extended and then irritated when I did not return at all. I never felt that he actually understood how sick I was.

Dr. Carter had long known that I abused drugs, and encouraged my action to enter treatment. At the same time, he (like most of my colleagues) knew little about the disease of addiction. During my months in psychotherapy with him, I had been outraged at him. I now recognize that he did the best he could at that time and I was outraged at everyone. He was a good doctor and a good psychiatrist.

I couldn't face Paul. I was enraged with him because I knew he must have had something to do with the intervention. I could not acknowledge at this time that the intervention was beneficial. All I could feel was fury that anyone would do this to me. I could not even bear to speak with Paul, so I left him a note before I left our house for the last time and took off for Atlanta.

I bought a one-way ticket to Atlanta and Ridgeview Institute. I had no expectations whatsoever that this treatment was different. I had no self, no hope. I came just to see, because I had no choice. I was just still breathing. Barely. I desperately needed a miracle.

Before I left for treatment, Connie handed me the first AA literature anybody ever put in my hands, the "Day by Day" book. She had inscribed it: "To Martha, because I love you. Connie, August 31, 1981." I remember her saying something about my being a drug addict; she was the first close friend who had ever described me as such. As she said it, I remember thinking, "She's known me all these years and she should know better."

11

THE MIRACLE BEGINS

Maggie put me on the plane early in the morning on Friday, September 11, 1981. I smoked a joint on the way to the airplane. Then Maggie and I indulged in some ham and eggs in one of those gross airport restaurants. I also ate some scopolamine to prevent travel sickness and threw in some Valium for good measure just before the plane took off. And of course I had a couple of drinks on the plane—a 7:00 A.M. flight. We weren't in the air more than fifteen minutes before I threw it all up.

Maggie Peters: I remember the day I took her to the airport. God, I don't know what possessed us to eat that terrible airport food. She did not want to go. She had all these wild plans, like going to Mexico and setting up a medical practice there. She thought she would go to Atlanta, play the game, and come home in a month.

Before she left, she gave me a whole bunch of stuff to put into a safety deposit box. We're talking junk! Shopping-list type garbage. But I trucked on down and put the stuff in the safety deposit box like it was valuable. I kept thinking, She has lost her mind if she is attached to this stuff.

After Martha left, I would send her long letters with articles from the newspapers, gags from Tampax ads, and items about the rising cost of lettuce—corn going down the poop chute of life. The articles had to do with what was happening in town, and I thought it would be good for her to stay in touch with her home.

I doubted that this so-called treatment would do me much good. I probably did blab on about starting a practice in Mexico, but, in fact, I was convinced that one way or another I was going to die. I wrote up a will and gave it to Maggie along with some sentimental possessions. I'm sure they looked like trash to her, but they were important to me, and I thought they would be meaningful to the recipients. For example, I willed my U. of A. pewter mug and plate to Eddie, my baseball card collection to Maggie's son, and a book entitled *Growing Mushrooms* to Maggie.

When we landed in Atlanta, I briefly considered remaining on the plane and flying on to Washington, D.C., but I forced myself to get off. Two impaired doctors—Jack, an anesthesiologist from Texas, and Tom, an ObGyn from Utah—were at the gate waiting for me. Both men were in their thirties and had been in treatment for several weeks.

As we drove the 30 miles to Ridgeview, Jack and Tom filled me in on the rules of the program in excruciating detail. Nevertheless, all I remember from our conversation was that I couldn't use drugs—including pot and alcohol—and I couldn't get involved in relationships with guys. I could understand (barely) that drugs would be forbidden in a treatment center, but the notion that pot and alcohol would be considered drugs seemed odd to me. Moreover, the idea that people in treatment were forbidden to get involved in relationships seemed absolutely bizarre. I didn't understand that idea at all, but at the same time, I couldn't fathom getting involved with a man at this point anyway. It was the furthest thing from my mind. My marriage was a mess—I had enough on my plate with an angry husband and a chaotic marriage.

To complicate my already confused state, not long into our journey from the airport to the hospital, the floorboard beneath my feet in the back seat of the car suddenly caught fire. Apparently the muffler had burned through. We made several stops at filling stations to deal with the fire, so it took three hours to get to Ridgeview, a drive that normally takes about forty-five minutes. We stocked up on about a dozen cans of soda, and I would pour Dr Pepper or Coke on the fire every time it blazed up.

Ridgeview is a richly endowed hospital, and as a result any depressing feeling of coldness normally associated with a psychiatric institution had been carefully obliterated. The hospital is made up of several small, modern buildings called cottages, which are beautifully designed and constructed of brick, glass, and rough-hewn wood, giving the entire hospital campus an atmosphere of light, airiness, warmth, and comfort. The receiving areas, offices, and rooms are painted in white and varying shades of rich blue and green, and are surprisingly comfortable. The grounds are manicured, but designed to look natural. Of course, when I entered Ridgeview, my terror prevented me from noticing any of this. I felt as if I were being locked up in Sing Sing.

Jack and Tom took me into the main reception area, a large ultra-modern, high-ceilinged room with sofas scattered around. I was admitted to Cottage A, the alcohol and drug treatment unit, and taken to my room, which I was to share with a twenty-one-year-old woman named Laura.

Again I was sort of taken aback. I had thought this was an impaired physicians program, not another hellhole for teenage junkies. I quickly learned that the general adult unit and the physicians unit were combined as far as sleeping, eating, some group therapy sessions, and most social activities were concerned. Thus, my roommate, Laura, who was admitted about the same time I was, was not a health professional; she was just a kid with a drug problem.

Laura was one of the youngest patients at Ridgeview, the daughter of a very wealthy businessman from Macon, Georgia. She had problems with Quaaludes, alcohol, and pot. As it turned out, we became fast friends, because I could relate better to a girl barely out of adolescence than to, say, a fifty-year-old alcoholic nurse.

On that first day I sat in my room for what seemed like hours, feeling bewildered, lost, and hideously angry. Finally, a couple of doctors came in and began to "debrief" me. I said I thought I probably needed to stop shooting dope, but I did not intend to stop smoking pot or drinking alcohol. I told them that I had been experimenting with, studying, and researching chemicals for more years than they could imagine. I knew my drugs. Over the years, I had always switched drugs and had not been physically addicted to any one of them. I said I was certain I would not experience drug withdrawal.

My denial was overwhelming. On one hand, I had made a serious and conscious effort to decrease my intake just before coming into treatment in order to minimize my discomfort. On the other hand, I honestly did not believe I would experience withdrawal. In fact, I truly did not feel that I was addicted, even as I sat on my bed, committed to a four-month drug treatment program.

One of the physicians, a guy who himself was in Phase III (outpatient professional placement) of treatment, took a drug history from me. I noticed that he wrote on my chart that I was an alcoholic as well as a drug addict. By now, I realized that they could make a case for my drug addiction, but I was astonished and offended that anyone would label me an alcoholic. I quickly assured him that he was wrong.

Of course, I began withdrawing almost immediately. Within hours, I became agitated and confused, and my whole body began to tremble. My blood pressure, heart rate, and respiration rose alarmingly. I became extremely paranoid, terrified of everyone and everything. I could not eat or sleep. By evening, the staff became so concerned about the level of my agitation and confusion that they put me on heavy doses of Tranxene and Valium, which theoretically allows you to come down (detoxify) more slowly. The detox measures did not help me much, yet I continued to insist that nothing was wrong, I wasn't having withdrawal, I would be fine.

Within twenty-four hours of entering treatment, virtually the first chemical-free hours I had known since the age of twelve, I became totally and grossly psychotic, utterly out of control. We were not supposed to use the telephone, but I needed to talk to Maggie, so I sneaked a call to her and begged her to come pick me up.

Maggie Peters: She called me on Friday night and begged me to get her out of there. She said they'd lied. The program was not for physicians; it was for the scum of the earth. She said regular people came there—it wasn't just for the elite dopey doctor.

I said, "I'm sorry, Martha. I'm just not going to come to get you. Tough shit. You're going to have to ride it out." The next day she hanged herself.

On Saturday night, I wrote a long letter to Maggie, which expressed my state of mind better than any recollection could. This letter was never mailed, and I found it about eight months later. The end of the letter just rails off in this funny handwriting and reveals how grossly psychotic I'd become in a few short hours. Here are some excerpts:

September 12, 1981
Dear Maggie—

Help me—God, help me. I feel like I might as well be naked and locked in the Quiet Room. It's not going to work. I cannot live without chemicals. I have a biochemical/genetically-based disease, or so they say. Horseshit. This goes against everything I've known from the street angle, patient angle, and professionally.

I have yet to see my doc yet and don't even know if it's Talbott. No phone calls, nothing for seven days. I almost shit. I asked to leave three hours after arrival, but they wouldn't let me. It's been 24 hours now.

Mag, I miss you. I needed to hear your voice last night. The people are nice. The docs are asses as usual, but most folks seem relatively comfortable, happy, and very satisfied with the program after the first 7 to 14 days. But I just don't know if I can make it. No phones—get this—no smoking in the rooms . . . I've been caught 4 times.

I have to be able to say I'm a drug addict and this program is based on four months' total abstinence, even from beer and pot. Before they let me leave for LOA (leave of absence), I have to be placed on Antabuse. I told them to shove it up their ass. I wouldn't do that. Lecture this morning says that's denial.

I've withdrawn, I cry continuously, I'm more agitated than ever, I can't buy this disease bullshit. There is no longer a light at the end of the tunnel. They require two year follow-ups and checks for total abstinence.

You are one of the most tremendous people I've known. I love you, Mag. I'm sorry to leave you alone.

— 149 —

*I can never stop taking drugs. I can't go on. Please
believe and be comforted in knowing that I've had a
hell of a short but intense life. After all, no one does
get out of here alive. Hang on to the good memories.
I'll either cut my throat or hang myself. So don't be
shocked. I'm sorry I'm such an asshole.*

I love you,
Martha

On Sunday morning, I went to a spiritual service they had at
the center, but it made me feel so guilty that I just left and
walked down into the beautiful wooded trails that surrounded
Ridgeview.

I found a fairly secluded place and knelt down and prayed
to God. I told God I knew I was the worst human being alive,
but I could suffer no longer and I could no longer cause others
to suffer. I asked him to forgive me and to take care of my
parents, Maggie, Connie, and my dogs. Immediately, a calm
and peaceful feeling came over me. I knew I was finally doing
the right thing.

I took off my belt and tied one end of it to a tree limb and
slipped the other end, which I had made into a noose, around
my neck. I then knelt down, hanging suspended from the tree
limb. The weight of my body forced pressure on both my
carotid arteries, shutting off the blood supply to my brain.
Then I lost consciousness. Apparently the knot slipped,
though, because the next thing I remember was coming to on
the ground. When I realized what had happened, I felt totally
humiliated. I had even screwed up my own suicide. I broke
down, scared out of my mind, totally out of control, unable to
think or reason. A few minutes later, two of my fellow patients
found me and led me back to Cottage A.

I was at an all-time low. I had finally gone as far as I could go
and still live. I was totally traumatized. I was still in this state

when, less than an hour later, I finally met Dr. G. Douglas Talbott, director of the Georgia Impaired Professionals Program.

Of course, a suicide attempt is serious business, and the staff had called Dr. Talbott the moment they found me. Yet, even as I sat there, shaken after attempting to take my own life, I would not surrender. I told Talbott that I was fine and demanded to leave treatment immediately. But he informed me that he was going to commit me to the psychiatric ward because I was suicidal, in severe drug withdrawal, and needed special care. No way was he going to let me leave. I told him he was full of shit, that I was a psychiatrist, more knowledgeable than anyone I'd ever met about drugs. I couldn't possibly be having withdrawal, and I really wasn't suicidal. It had all been a mistake.

In reality, I was virtually insane—a common secondary symptom of severe drug withdrawal.

G. Douglas Talbott: I had heard about Martha two years before she came for treatment. One of the people from the University of Arkansas had told me that one of the psychiatric residents was in trouble. The problem was not with her work; the problem was that she was using drugs away from work. It wasn't until after she'd been at Ridgeview for a month or six weeks that I remembered that conversation and put it all together.

In fact, I don't think most of the people concerned with Martha's residency were aware of her problem at all. It's not unusual for physicians to be unaware of addiction in themselves or in their colleagues. Clearly, physicians are often deeply in trouble, but it doesn't usually show up at work in doctors until the very end, until they are extremely ill.

Part of the reason addiction or alcoholism doesn't show up in doctors is because doctors are often able to hide the problem. But the real issue is the diplomas on the wall—they're sacred. Doctors will abstain in such a way as to prevent addiction from interfering with their work until it is completely, rampantly out of control. They—we—say, "I can't be an alcoholic because booze doesn't interfere with my work." Yet it has probably been taking a toll outside of work—at home, with our health, and in our social life. By the time addiction reaches the work arena with a physician or nurse, it is terminal—it is end stage.

I first saw Martha a couple of days after her admission when she tried to commit suicide. By that time, I had a staff of doctors, and they would bring me only the problem cases. Other people were also taking care of Martha at the time, but I took her under my wing and ultimately kept her as my private patient.

Talbott, the famous doc who was supposed to save me, locked me up in Cottage B, the psychiatric ward, on suicide precautions. At this point, I almost didn't care. I was so nuts that I couldn't figure out how to escape, manipulate them into letting me leave, or even make another suicide attempt. As a result of my withdrawal, I began hallucinating and was more psychotically paranoid than ever. Until now, I had always been able to attribute my hallucinations, delusions, and paranoia to drugs. But I wasn't taking drugs now, and yet all this was happening—which flipped me out. Therefore, the personal diagnosis I'd come to six months before, when I'd cut out most of my drugs for five days, was clinched: I was nuts. I wasn't crazy because of drugs, I was just crazy. For years the drugs had allowed me to fool the world. I was terrified of mental illness, and the notion that I was out of control was the most frightening thing I could imagine.

Dr. Talbott tried to reason with me during those early days. He said of course I was crazy, but I was crazy from the years of taking drugs, nothing else. I thought, Oh, sure. I figured that only I could know how truly crazy I was. After all, I was a psychiatrist. Talbott told me I had to remember that I was withdrawing, not from any one drug, or just from those I had been taking prior to admission, but from seventeen years of hard-core, malignant, daily chemical use. I didn't believe a word of it.

I remember very little about my week-long stay on the psychiatric ward. In fact, I recall very little about the early stages of treatment. Initially I felt that my already disintegrated world had totally collapsed. Here I was, 800 miles from home, totally alone and isolated, not knowing or understanding what was happening to me, locked up in a nut ward, utterly crazy. I wanted to do the only thing I knew how to do, needed to do in order to survive—take drugs.

Communicating with Maggie became one of my few links with reality, and I wrote to her almost every day. Sometimes I didn't mail the letters, but used them as sort of a diary, as I had done years before.

September 13, 1981
Dear Mag—

I just tried to phone you. I tried to hang myself. What an asshole. I wish you were here to stone me and make me carry the cross. I'm such a fool. So now I'm on the crazy ward.

They want me to "surrender" to a "higher power"—God, or whatever, they're not specific. In other words, give up the little control I've got left. What shit. You know very well how I am about control.

You were right—it's not as bad as I expected. It's worse. I'm on suicide precautions, so I can't get glass, wire, string. No drugs. I cry a lot. It's hopeless.

— 153 —

Maybe I really should be here (crazy house).

I am withdrawing, incredible as it may seem. This whole thing is unreal. I'm a persistent fuck-up—how could I have let all this happen? They say I'm "not responsible." They tell all the families that, too. Jesus, I'm lonely—have been for a long time, but this is really alone. I have great difficulty, as you know, asking for help, let alone just talking to these people. They say the disease is responsible. What B.S.

How can I possibly resolve all this? This morning I said, "Never." I thought of you and asked God or whoever to make it easier for you. Then I smoked two cigs in place of my last supper. Then I had this strange calm, tied my belt to a tree after slipping it through the buckle, and hanged myself.

Strange high, sort of chokes you up (no pun intended), but stars, lights, almost euphoria. Knot slipped and I passed out on the ground. I couldn't bring myself to run onto the freeway, so I returned finally to the cottage. I was a wreck. It scared me, Mag. I've always known I'd commit suicide, but, Jesus God, to try to hang myself.

I need help. I may have to really get it. I want to come back right now. The moods change so rapidly. You've seen me as depressed as anyone. I love you.

Martha

Years later, I read the medical evaluations that were written during the eight days I was on Cottage B, by Talbott, two other doctors, and a social worker. Each professional wrote up my "life story" in great detail. It amazed me that somehow I had been able to provide so much information about myself while I was in an acute state of withdrawal. But the most interesting observations are their interpretations of my life and of my emotional and social state.

ADDICTIVE DISEASE ASSESSMENT, G. Douglas Talbott,
Attending Physician, September 19, 1981

This twenty-nine-year-old white married psychiatric resident
from Arkansas Medical School in Little Rock is being transferred back to the alcohol and drug unit from the psychiatric
unit. She was hospitalized (on the psychiatric ward) for a few
days as a result of severe withdrawal symptoms from polydrug
addiction, with Demerol and cocaine as her drugs of choice.
She had expressed some suicidal ideation, and Dr. Udel and I
both thought it would be better to transfer her to B unit. . . .

When you ask Dr. Morrison—and it is interesting that she is
now using her maiden name—to list drugs she has used, the
list she provides is tantamount to the *PDR (Physicians Desk
Reference)*. She states without any question that her drugs of
choice arc I.V. Demerol mixcd with cocaine, but she has used
almost every drug in the book. She is a street junkie with the
wisdom resulting from many years of drug use, drug abuse,
and drug addiction. . . .

PHYSICAL HEALTH: Shc is grossly underweight and is con-
ccrned about her inability to put on weight. She is not aware
of any specific organ disease, and except for being poorly
nourished, her physical exam is within normal limits. . . .

ADDICTIVE DISEASE PROGRAMS/INTERVENTIONS: Pa-
tient has serious professional problems. Also, her marital problems are severe. This is her second marriage. Her husband is
thirty years older. They have been separated for two months,
and she has tremendously ambivalent feelings toward him. He
witnessed and cared for her during several severe drug overdoses.

Patient obviously has a tremendous degree of embarrassment, shame, and guilt as a result of her continued drug intake. Consequently, she has had a severe loss of self-esteem.

Intervention with the process is going to depend on educating her about the disease of chemical dependency and providing her with nonchemical coping skills as an alternative to the mood-altering drugs.

DISCUSSION: This patient shows a combination of tremendous guilt and tremendous anger, particularly toward her present husband. There is no question that her chemical dependency is severe. Because of her seventeen-year history with this disease, she has suffered severe maturation arrest, particularly in emotional development, socialization, leisure time, and communication skills. Dr. Morrison has great difficulty trusting people because of her own lack of self-esteem. It is going to be important to get her to become involved in Alcoholics Anonymous and Narcotics Anonymous, so that the self-help groups can not only help her find nonchemical coping skills, but also help her learn to trust people and stay open. Communication, openness, and sharing are going to be critical to her recovery.

SOCIAL HISTORY, Diane Fitzgerald, M.S.W., September 18, 1981

Martha Morrison is a twenty-nine-year-old separated female admitted to Cottage A for drug abuse on September 11, 1981. After an attempted suicide while the patient was in withdrawal from drugs, she was transferred to Cottage B on September 13. Patient was referred by Dr. Harvey Irwin from the Impaired Physicians Committee in Arkansas. Patient is a senior resident in psychiatry and is in her first year of fellowship in child and adolescent psychiatry. The patient is admitted for the Impaired Professionals Program and will return to Cottage A once the withdrawal and suicidal ideation have subsided.

PRESENTING PROBLEM AND HISTORY: [Diane wrote one of the most detailed histories of a patient I'd ever seen. It went on for more than ten typewritten pages. As I've said, I was somehow able to relate my life story to her quite factually and clearly, and she took it down year by year and drug by drug. Here are the drugs I told her about, which Diane carefully listed.]

1964: Darvon.

1967: Tobacco, alcohol.

1969: Pot, Darvon, alcohol, non-prescribed cough medicines, hash, LSD, mescaline, Preludin, crystal, Dilaudid, amphetamine sulfate, tobacco.

1970: Amphetamines, tobacco, Seconal, LSD, peyote, Talwin, Dexamyl, Benzedrine, pot, Dilaudid, Demerol, codeine, pentobarbital, Tuinal, alcohol, cough syrup, Valium, Contac, morphine, cocaine, Preludin, Desoxyn, amphetamine sulfate, MDA, STP, psilocybin, Darvon, hash, opium, Tofranil, and Mellaril.

1971–74: Cocaine, Seconal, Tuinal, pentobarbital, Dilaudid, Demerol, THC, alcohol, pot, hash, morphine, methadone, heroin, opium, Talwin, Darvon, Quaaludes, Valium, speed with addiction to opium and Demerol.

1975–76: Pot, alcohol, heroin, coke, Demerol, Dilaudid, codeine, morphine, Mellaril.

1977: Codeine, pot, alcohol, morphine, heroin, coke, Mellaril.

1978: Codeine, coke, Demerol, pot, alcohol—and received the Upjohn Achievement Award.

1979: Codeine, coke, Demerol, Mepergan—overdosed on Demerol and won the Outstanding Intern of the Year Award.

1980: Codeine, coke, pot, alcohol, amphetamines, prescribed Elavil, Tagamet, antacids, Mepergan.

1981: Codeine, coke, Mepergan, Demerol, pot, alcohol, Ritalin, Tylox, Percodan, opium, amphetamines, Fastin, Cogentin, Artane, Stress Tabs, Ativan.

RECOMMENDATIONS: I recommend the twenty-nine-day alcohol and drug treatment program and Phase II (outpatient, halfway house) of the Impaired Professionals Program. I would also recommend that perhaps this patient receive extended treatment beyond the normal four months recommended for most of the doctors in the program. I suggest a family assessment to determine the condition of the patient's marriage. Referral to aftercare services and continual and ongoing treatment through Narcotics Anonymous and Alcoholics Anonymous. Patient plans to return to her therapist upon discharge.

PSYCHIATRIC CONSULTATION, Mel Udel, M.D., September 14, 1981

FINDINGS: Patient is a twenty-nine-year-old white married female psychiatric resident from Little Rock, Arkansas, referred by Dr. Harvey Irwin for treatment of polydrug dependence. Patient has a long malignant history of chemical dependence (polydrug) as well as psychiatric disorders and hospitalizations since early adolescence. She has used every known common addictive chemical by every route of entry and, associated with this, has been hospitalized three times in psychiatric hospitals with various diagnoses of affective-type disorders. But she was always using chemicals, so it is not possible to unscramble the history.

MENTAL STATUS: Looks quiet, downcast; speech relevant, logical, coherent. Mood: Depressed, and affect appropriate. Thought: No evidence of thinking disorder, but content appropriate to depression. Sensorium and intellect: Intact, lacks insight into chemical nature of affective disorder, attributes to psyche.

DIAGNOSIS: 1. Organic brain syndrome, secondary to withdrawal, with depression. 2. Chemical dependence, polydrug.

RECOMMENDATION: 1. Keep in Cottage B (psychiatric) for

control and observation. 2. When stabilized, return to Impaired Professionals Program, Cottage A. 3. Psychologic testing in four to six weeks. 4. With this history, she will probably need an extended program to recover.

PSYCHOLOGICAL EVALUATION, Tom Butcher, Ph.D.
September 25, 1981

PERSONALITY DESCRIPTION: This is a complex and intense young woman who finds the process of opening herself emotionally to others intensely difficult. She is presently struggling hard to save her life, although she has suicidal fantasies and occasional suicidal attempts that are genuine efforts to end her life. Her personality structure is quite interesting; there is a long-term intense struggle against feelings of inadequacy and incompetence. She is out to show herself capable of doing everything with an extremely high level of competence, and she is generally quite capable of doing so.

Feelings are an intense experience for her and are perceived as motions of energy which dramatically influence her internal experience and her external behavior. She welcomes this intensity, enjoys it, and longs for it in its absence. This longing is connected with her use of chemicals, as these chemicals serve the purpose of reducing internal controls and leaving her more accessible to the intense waves of feeling. She presently sees long-term abstinence as a major threat to her ability to experience the waves of pleasure, but this is a groundless fear, and she will be able to experience considerable pleasure and satisfaction only with sober experience behind her.

TEST RESULTS: The Wechsler shows excellent intellectual ability. There is no indication of deterioration, and immediate memory and capacity to retain new information are both excellent. Abstract thinking, problem-solving ability, and perception of fine detail are particularly advanced here.

The Figure Drawings show a high level of anxiety, fears that she will be unacceptable to other people, together with some problems in identification. She apparently tries to live with a minimum of contact between herself and the world around her, makes efforts to conceal much of her inner life from others, and is generally quite successful in doing so.

The projective techniques, Rorschach and MMPI, show a very complex woman with strong masochistic features. She places a high level of demand upon herself, becomes quickly irritated with authority and control, and sets about finding her own means for avoiding controls. Emotional experience is intense and she is not particularly interested in controlling her feelings or suppressing them. She feels herself basically to be quite different from other people and expects rejection and disapproval from them should they see her clearly and distinctly.

This is a very complex woman, suicidal intention is real, and she occasionally becomes so overwhelmed by her intense feelings that she will act on these suicidal fantasies. There is evidence for a masculine identification or at least some sexual confusion.

Diagnostic impression is (1) chemical addiction, (2) schizophrenic reaction, latent type with an overlay personality disorder showing paranoid and sociopathic features. Occasional suicidal efforts are a distinct possibility, but there is a great deal of resource and strength available in this woman's personality. Long-term prognosis looks good.

RECOMMENDATIONS: The main part of the problem at present is to encourage, promote, and allow her to open herself and her inner experience to other people. In particular, she needs to talk about her intense-feeling experiences and to develop some idea that pleasure and intensity are available to her even though she remains abstinent.

On September 19, after the suicide precautions had been discontinued, I was allowed to return to the alcohol and drug cottage, and the room I shared with Laura. I was slightly relieved since I preferred to be among psychotic drug addicts rather than psychotic psychotics.

Each day I experienced more withdrawal symptoms—shakes, tremors, agitation, confusion, hallucinations, and paranoia. I had marked difficulty talking, thinking, and reasoning. For a while, I was almost catatonic, very withdrawn, and paranoid. I would just sit and hallucinate. I didn't talk because I couldn't pull my thoughts together. What's more, I was afraid that if I said anything, the staff would know how insane I was and send me back to the psychiatric cottage.

After about ten days, I began to attend all of the treatment lectures and group therapy sessions that formed the core of the treatment program. From 8:15 A.M. to 5:30 P.M., each minute was carefully accounted for. We had a nondenominational inspirational service each morning for thirty minutes, followed by an hour-long drug and alcohol education lecture. From 10:00 to 11:15, we went to an on-campus general Alcoholics Anonymous or Narcotics Anonymous meeting, and immediately afterward we attended a one-hour peer group therapy session. (Peer group, at Ridgeview, could mean men's group, women's group, doctors' group—whatever was appropriate.)

After a short lunch break, we'd have a general group therapy meeting for one hour, followed by a lecture on coping skills. From 4:00 to 5:00 we were permitted one hour of exercise or gym followed by a specialty meeting of some sort, like art therapy or a young adult meeting.

During the evening hours we were also carefully monitored. Twice a week we were required to go to an off-campus AA or NA meeting. On other evenings we were permitted to have visitors or to read or socialize for a couple of hours. On most evenings, we also were required to attend a lecture of some sort, an AA speakers meeting, or other AA- or NA-related meetings. These meetings usually followed the "free time," so that the staff could observe the patients' whereabouts and state of mind before they went to bed at the wild and crazy hour of 9:30.

On weekends, we had more so-called free time, but it was always a planned activity of some kind or monitored visiting hours. Of course, I did not participate in these activities with the enthusiasm of a Razorback cheerleader. I had no choice; attendance was mandatory, but I was beginning to accept my lack of control.

Each week, the "impaired docs" were required to attend five groups designed especially for physicians and other health professionals. The Caduceus meeting, the best known of the impaired physicians groups and the focal point of the program, was held on Tuesday evenings. It was an intense, confrontational group designed for and attended by addicted or alcoholic doctors in treatment, including outpatients. Immediately following the Caduceus meeting, we were required to attend an International Doctors in AA meeting, which, despite its name, was open to all health professionals. On Thursday afternoons, we had a group therapy session especially for doctors who were in active treatment. On Saturday mornings, we had a group that included all health professionals—not only doctors, but nurses, technicians, and others—and was open to all "recovering" health professionals whether they were in the hospital, in outpatient treatment, or just in need of group support. Immediately following this meeting there was a family therapy meeting to which parents, spouses, and children of "recovering" health professionals were allowed to come for lectures and Al-Anon-type therapy.

These health professional groups, designed and instituted by Doug Talbott, were the very meetings that made Ridgeview and Talbott's Impaired Professionals Program legendary and unique. The doctors' groups tend to focus on professional issues relating to doctors; but more, they are far more confrontational than the general therapy groups because doctors possess a much greater system of denial.

Most doctors find it almost impossible to be patients. Because they possess extensive medical knowledge and because they are used to saving everybody else's life, doctors simply will not listen to a business executive or a housewife confront them about their health. In fact, it's a lucky day if they will listen to another doctor's advice. When you add to this factor the denial that accompanies any addiction, you have a wall of resistance that is almost impossible to scale.

Of course, the purpose of the Impaired Professionals Program is to break down this wall, to force addicted doctors to face their disease, to forge through their denial, and to make them listen to the advice of their professional peers and of others who are familiar with addiction. In a successful therapeutic situation, doctors are not separated from other patients because such a division isn't realistic. For that reason, the docs and the other patients at Ridgeview live together and share in a number of groups. But particularly in the initial stages of treatment, it is very important for one addicted doctor to have the support of another addicted doctor.

Because my disease was so malignant and because my innate resistance was so intense, I didn't feel that I fit into any of the groups, professional or general. I was younger than most of the other patients, I was the only resident, and I was the only female doctor in the place. The problem was even more complex because I was a strange mixture of hot-shot superstar resident and bottom-line street junkie.

Most of these docs hadn't gotten addicted until they'd been out in private practice, so they'd been using "clean" drugs. Why shoot heroin bought from some scumbag off the street when you can pass a respectable script for Demerol or codeine? Why guzzle Ripple, panhandled from some skid row drunk, when you can pull up to a store in your BMW, stock up on Johnnie Walker Black, and drink it in the privacy of your own home? These guys were rarely out copping dope on the street from some slimeball they wouldn't walk within thirty paces of in a normal situation.

I'd been forging scripts, ripping off drugstores, and firing up dope for eight years before I entered med school, and I didn't feel comfortable around all these doctors, with their uppity professional bullshit. I had never liked that sort of thing, drugs or no drugs; rubbing elbows with the upper class was just not me. What's more, part of me always got off on the shock value of being with the hippies and the degenerates. I fit in better with them than I did with the doctors. Later, as I gained my sobriety and I felt more comfortable with my own professionalism, I could relate to the doctors, but that maturity didn't develop for months.

Not surprisingly, I fit in best, at least during the early stages of treatment, at the Narcotics Anonymous meetings. On Monday, September 21, ten days after I arrived, I attended my first open Narcotics Anonymous meeting, which was held at an off-campus building in Marietta, Georgia. The meeting room was filled with a bunch of old hippie, street-shooting dope fiends who rode up on their fat hog motorcycles. These were hard-core guys, and I understood them. For the first time, I heard two slogans that made tremendous sense to me: "One is never enough and a thousand is too many," and "We live to use and we use to live." These two statements were the story of my life. I easily accepted that I, too, was a dope fiend, and I knew for the first time in my life that I was right where I belonged. They told me they loved me, and they asked me to keep coming back. And I did.

A week later, on Monday, September 28, I attended my first open off-campus Alcoholics Anonymous meeting, which was also attended by Smyrna residents. The AA meeting was more difficult for me, not because of my professional status, which was often the barrier for other doctors, but because while I accepted that I was a hard-core drug addict, I still did not believe that I was an alcoholic. More problematically, I was not able to wholeheartedly commit myself to the most basic agreement of NA and AA: to not drink or take drugs again. I was willing to abstain at this particular time, I was willing to come to meetings, and I was willing to try to stop dying. But I could not yet honestly commit myself to a life without drugs.

By the end of September, after three weeks in the program, my brain had cleared just enough for me to begin to comprehend how very ill I was. I had always done everything with the help of drugs—everything. Now I was expected to do all the things normal people did—walk, talk, eat, bathe, dress, interact, think—without drugs. And I didn't know how. This alone was a remarkable realization. And it terrified me.

For several weeks, I literally could not eat, sleep, or change my clothes by myself. I would try to put on clean clothes and find that I couldn't get them buttoned or zipped, so I would walk around for days wearing the same overalls and dirty T-shirt, smelling like a locker room. I would decide to go to lunch, walk out of my room, and forget where I was going. I couldn't find my way to group therapy meetings, so I wouldn't go or I'd show up late. I would have liked to put on a clean shirt or eat a sandwich, but acting on these everyday impulses was impossible for me.

To the staff, I appeared to be resisting, and certainly there was a ferocious strain of rebelliousness in my attitude. They'd tell me to take a bath, and I'd have a fit. They'd yell at me for missing a meeting, and I'd have a temper tantrum. They'd scream at me for wandering off, and I'd scream right back. But underlying my childlike, regressive behavior was a feeling of sheer terror; I couldn't help it. I just couldn't help it.

On several occasions, Talbott and I had violent arguments. I'd tell him he didn't know a damn thing about drugs, that his disease concept was bullshit, and that his treatment program sucked. He would tell me to stop acting like a two-year-old. I could get better, he said, but it was going to take time because I was so sick. At one point, he threatened to lock me up in Cottage B for sixty days if I didn't behave. I felt bludgeoned, but the threat of the psycho ward had an effect.

G. Douglas Talbott: Martha had what is called a "camel hump withdrawal." She went through an acute withdrawal, leveled out, and then went into a second withdrawal ten days to two weeks later, which is why I call it the camel hump. This second withdrawal often happens with addiction to cocaine and some of the stimulants. Often people become disoriented and then dysfunctional.

Martha was wild when she arrived. She was a very sick lady and it was difficult dealing with her. However, I can relate to people in this state because I can remember the pain of my own addiction. I was impressed with how empty she felt, how frightened and lonely she was, and how hopeless she perceived herself to be. She was a challenge.

One night in early October during a restless, tumultuous few hours of something I would not define as sleep, I actually wet the bed. On several occasions, I had had severe sweats and chills, and my bedclothes had been drenched, but in this instance, there was no mistaking the dampness. The sweats and chills had been humiliating enough, but wetting the bed totally shamed me. Nevertheless, I still did not realize that I was experiencing protracted withdrawal.

On another occasion, much to my amazement and horror, I experienced something like delirium tremens. For several hours one night, I lay in my bed, unable to move or call out, trying to pick what felt like spiders, flat worms, and black roaches out of my clothes and hair. They seemed to be all over me, crawling up my nose and into my mouth. For hours, I hovered in a dreamlike state, half in and half out of consciousness, and when I finally came to, I was soaking wet and absolutely terrified.

After a few weeks of treatment, I also began to experience physical complications as a result of my chronic addiction and malnutrition. For starters, my teeth began to literally rot out of my head. I had one tooth removed; then the one next to it became abscessed and reabscessed. I had two root canal treatments, but I finally lost that tooth, also. All of this occurred during two weeks in October, and the pain of the abscesses on top of the pain of my withdrawal—not to mention my emotional torment—was too much. I wanted to die.

Yet, as I was regressing physically, emotionally, and behaviorally, I was able, at least intellectually, to make a little sense of it. I wrote my thoughts in my diary in early October.

> *I'm relatively empty and numb. My biggest fear is loss of control . . . yet I crossed the wall into addiction as an adolescent and lost real control many years ago. Guilt, fear, anger, and depression are very real to me, and loneliness is definitely my assassin. There is no question regarding the extent of my addiction and no other cause except my disease. A significant problem is that absolutely everything is a trigger mechanism for me to use drugs. God help me, because for all practical purposes, I have never been straight and I'm scared. It took me over half my life of pure hell to get here, and it's hell to get out. I don't really know what I can do or what I can't do. I don't really know what I feel or don't feel. I have to want to get well; I'm desperately exhausted from dying, and terrified of living with or without drugs.*
>
> *I'm glad I'm here.*

On October 6, almost a month after my arrival at Ridgeview, I gave my "pilgrimage." Giving a pilgrimage means that a patient writes her life story and then reads it to her fellow patients during a general (nonprofessional) group therapy session. The purpose of the pilgrimage is to allow each patient to relate his or her history and to force the patients to consider how the medical, social, and psychological aspects of their addiction have affected their lives. For the first time, I began to piece together certain incidents, relationships, and attitudes I had carried with me all my life and finally make some sense of them.

I realized that my addiction had caused numerous physical problems for me. It was while I was preparing my pilgrimage that I remembered the incident with my friend, Joanie, when I fell out of bed in a crazy drunken state and cracked my head open. I also remembered an event from 1972 when, while stoned, I fell on some ice and hyperextended my thumb. I splinted it myself even though I was in undergraduate school at the time, not a trained physician. Five years later, during my senior year in med school, my thumb became virtually useless. I had it x-rayed and discovered that the ligament had never healed properly. I had it operated on and, for a time, thought that my thumb joint might have to be fused completely.

I recalled several automobile accidents I'd had while drunk or high. In one case, I was driving left-footed (and barefoot) because I'd lacerated my right foot in a motorcycle accident (also barefoot, also high) a few days before. I had shot up Preludin and barbs, drunk a fifth of Southern Comfort, smoked a load of pot, and hopped into my dad's car. I turned a corner and my foot slipped off the brake and onto the accelerator. I ran full tilt into a tree and totaled the car. I lacerated my forehead, bruised my ribs, wrecked my knees, and generally felt as if I'd been run over by a semi. My friends called my father, who towed the car away. I refused to be taken to the emergency room and ended up looking like a hydrocephalic for two weeks, with a swelled head and two black eyes.

I remembered the uncountable episodes of septicemia, the overdoses—particularly the heroin overdose with Jake and the Demerol overdose with Paul, and the unexplainable stomach problems and headaches. For the first time, I was able to rationally explain my blackouts. In fact, it was only during treatment that I learned about the phenomenon of blacking out. I remembered the years I secretly believed I was insane because I had forgotten a conversation or lost track of time. I was astonished to learn this was because of the drugs. I also was appalled at the energy I'd expended inventing excuses and alibis for my blackouts and realized the toll the compensating had taken on my peace of mind and self-esteem. For the first time, I realized that almost all of the physical pain and much of the psychological pain I had endured in my life was a result of drug addiction. It was almost impossible for me to take this in. As distressing as this realization was, it was also something of a relief to know that it wasn't me; it was the dope.

I found it even more disturbing to come to terms with details of my family life, particularly my marital relationships. The link between drugs and my marriage to Brad was painfully obvious—two lonesome junkies looking for salvation. My marriage to Paul was more upsetting, partly because I was still in it, but more because although I was aware of the horror of our marriage, I had not considered—had not been able to consider—how insidiously pathological our relationship actually was. Drugs had destroyed our marriage as surely as they had killed my marriage to Brad. Paul was not an addict, but he was a classic "enabler"—the significant person who unconsciously attempts to protect and control the addict, succeeding only in allowing the addiction to continue.

I also learned much about my relationship to my parents. Unwittingly, and surely out of love, they, too, had enabled me.

During my pilgrimage, I told the others about my conflicts with my mother and my blind adoration of my dad. I had been aware of my anger toward my mother since my adolescent psychiatric treatment, but now I began to perceive anger toward my dad as well. I had always thought he was the disciplinarian, but in reality it had been my mother. They had supported me, particularly during my teenage drug episodes, but often they, too, had enabled me—like the time Daddy towed the totaled car and agreed not to take me to the hospital. Only once did they give up on me, when they insisted that I move out of their house during college because they could not endure my being strung out. Even then, they allowed me to live rent-free in the Fallin Street apartment, and they turned a blind eye to my drug activities.

At the same time, as I began to recover, my guilt toward my parents intensified. My addiction had affected them markedly. I had seen my father turn gray within a year of my initial hospitalization, and I saw now that my mother's compulsive nagging about my drinking and her secret searches for drugs had stemmed from fear and love, not from disapproval. I saw clearly how much they loved me, and I realized how helpless they must have felt for years.

Much to my amazement, my pilgrimage revealed to me how much love and loyalty I had always received from my friends. Old friends like Sally, Joanie, and Connie had stuck by me despite my obsession with dope and my frequent inability to reciprocate their attentions. Maggie, a relatively new friend, had been equally devoted throughout my illness.

G. Douglas Talbott: Martha was very bright. I wasn't concerned with permanent brain damage from the drugs. I also saw that she had an incredible capacity to reach out to people and to relate to people, if she could trust them, but she had a terrible time, initially, trusting people.

Then, of course, there was this intangible quality—she was

a very warm and soft person underneath. She covered this up with a lot of bravado and macho stuff when she came in. A lot of hostile stuff, a lot of four-letter words, but underneath, I saw a lot of gentleness and warmth. She became like a surrogate daughter to me.

By early October, I began to perceive that I was making some headway. At this point, it was only a hazy glimmer of hope, but I saw it. I continued to have difficulty relating to others and to the program of recovery, so I wrote—letters, poems, diary entries—mostly because it was easier for me to put my thoughts on paper than to express them orally. One poem reveals the forcefulness of the hope that was beginning to develop inside me.

INSIGHT
You've got to keep fighting
for your life.
Don't you ever give in!
It's such a simple suicide
Letting the needle win.
Don't let the needle win!

12
MIDNIGHT SUNRISE

Alcoholism and drug addiction are diseases.
They are treatable.
With the grace of God, there is hope for recovery.
                    MARTHA MORRISON, 1984

The first time I heard Dr. Doug Talbott give the "disease concept" lecture, I was in shock. This man might as well have been telling my life story—the progression of the illness, the loss of control, the denial, the confusion, the paranoia, the guilt, the embarrassment, the withdrawal, and the terrible loneliness. He had answers to some of the "whys" that I had never understood, like why I continued to take drugs despite the horrendous consequences.

According to Talbott, the disease concept is based on the premise that addicts are born with a genetic abnormality or, in other words, the inherited potential to respond in an abnormal or allergic fashion to mood-altering chemicals. People born with this type of genetic predisposition exhibit neuro-chemical imbalances and deficiencies, and become addicted if their system is challenged with any type of mood-altering chemical, regardless of the chemical or the dosage. In addition, the liver, which normally metabolizes or breaks down most drugs, functions in a very unusual fashion in these people, producing chemicals that cause the addict to respond differently to alcohol or drugs. These biochemical abnormalities in the brain and liver are responsible for the compulsive craving that leads to repeated use of a drug, despite negative consequences. Willpower has no influence whatsoever.

The disease process also has recognizable psychological and social consequences. To put it simply, once the disease takes hold, the addict ceases to care about anything except his drug of choice. All personal relationships break down, marriages fall apart, work becomes impossible, and careers are ruined. The addict's personal sense of self becomes utterly distorted as he or she descends further into the grip of the drug. In the end, unless it is treated, the disease ends in death.

Doug Talbott was not the "author," so to speak, of the disease concept, but he was one of the first doctors to adapt the concept to a treatment setting, and he was a leader in the use of the disease concept in the treatment of addicted doctors.

At first I didn't believe a word of it. This concept went totally against my training as a scientist. Nevertheless, astonishing as it seemed at the time, I began to realize that doctors could be—God forbid—wrong. Most physicians accepted the moralistic view concerning drug addiction and alcoholism. They saw it as moral deprivation, a "weakness of character." According to them, junkies were junkies and drunks were drunks because they wanted to be. All they had to do to get over their addiction was exercise a little self-control and willpower. Through Talbott, I learned that addicts didn't lack willpower; they suffered from a disease.

I realized that if I was going to survive this hell, I had to believe in someone. That someone turned out to be Doug Talbott. For the first time, I had met someone who stood up to me. When he talked with me, I felt—again for the first time— that he actually understood what I had been through. It was as if he could read my mind, which, of course, also made me more paranoid, but his empathy gave me some relief. Here was another human being who really seemed to understand the depths of my despair and who could relate to it and to me. I felt a bond I had never had with anyone. He was the first person I really began to trust.

Initially, Talbott became my Higher Power, the being I submitted to in the belief that he could save me. I believed he was a power greater than myself. Fortunately, very fortunately for me, he never violated that trust. I believe this was a necessary step for me in the journey of my recovery and in the development of my concept of a true Higher Power and the God of my understanding.

Throughout treatment and a great part of my recovery, Doug Talbott held my hand, guided me, and directed me to the best of his ability. This was no small task and required a consummate amount of energy, time, and love. I really don't know why he took such an interest in me. I suppose he really was able to perceive something in me that others couldn't see. I also suspect that with my personality, my particular accomplishments, and the malignancy of my disease, I was something of a mirror image of himself.

G. Douglas Talbott: I was raised in Dayton, Ohio, and I had a very ordinary family life—except that my mother was often missing. She was alcoholic. She never abused us or embarrassed us; she just gradually started drinking more and more, and finally disappeared from family life.

I went to prep school at Hotchkiss in Lakeville, Connecticut, as my family had done for generations, and after graduation I immediately went to Yale. Due to the war, I went through Yale in about fourteen months. In June 1943, I went to New Haven, and in June 1944, I moved down to the med school at Columbia Physicians and Surgeons in New York City.

I drank, probably for the first time, during med school. During my sophomore year of med school I got drunk at a social gathering. Much later it was clear to me that when I drank, I never drank for the occasion, I drank for the feeling the alcohol gave me, and I drank until I got that feeling.

After med school, I finished one year's internship, then five years of residency at the University of California, where I was chief resident in medicine. Internal medicine and cardiology were my specialties. I also got married during med school to a lovely woman, Polly, in 1947. Being good Catholics, we began having kids right away and eventually had six altogether.

During the Korean War, I joined the Air Force. I became medical director of a military hospital in Dayton, Ohio, and then quickly, personal medical aide to the Secretary of the Air Force and to the Chief of Staff of the Air Force.

As a result of my connection with Air Force officials, I got into the Washington scene. They'd call me, and I'd do things like go over to the White House and give David Eisenhower his polio shot. Those were party days.

In the late 1950s, I joined up with Terry McGuire from the Mayo Clinic and Randy Lovelace from the Lovelace Clinic in Albuquerque, and we designed and initiated the medical component of the Mercury astronaut program. I was a civilian consultant in charge of crew selection and fitness training for the original seven astronauts in the Mercury program.

This was big-time, but it was also party time. I began to drink pretty heavily at parties during this time, but by then you couldn't tell me anything. I was one of the most highly trained doctors in the country, and my career was going great. I was in control.

After I left the astronaut program, I took my training and technical knowledge and melded it into my private cardiology practice in Dayton, Ohio. Working with General Electric, IBM, and the Cox family, I helped build the first computerized coronary care unit in the country, and started The Cox Heart Institute, where I served as director.

By then, Polly and I had our six kids and a marvelous home

in Dayton. Everything was great, except that I was working very hard, and when I came home late at night, I got into the habit of having a drink or two or three to relax.

Then I began playing chemical ping-pong with a pill known as Equanil. If I was feeling tense or on one of my "I'm not drinking" binges, I would take a few tranquilizers or an injection instead of a drink.

Over an incredibly short time, I developed true alcoholism, with all the characteristics of the disease—the hidden bottles, the inability to stop, the denial. I didn't know I was alcoholic, and of course nobody would accept that the fair-haired boy was a drunk. Finally the drinking interfered with my work to such an extent that in 1967 I was fired from Cox. Over the preceding three years, I had been hospitalized twenty-two times—never for alcoholism, of course—always for flu, rectal bleeding, or some other malady that actually resulted from the drinking. When I was fired, I was devastated; but more, I didn't know what to do.

My denial was massive. I knew something was wrong, and for a while, I thought I was schizophrenic or suffering from some other psychiatric problem. So, for the next two years, I tried treatment at a psychiatric hospital in Columbus, Ohio, only to be declared "hopeless." At no time did they suggest that I might be alcoholic.

By now it was 1969. I was still drinking. I had six kids. I was up to my ass in mortgages. So I decided to take a job in an emergency room in San Francisco. I couldn't sell my house in Dayton, so my family stayed behind, and I was hideously lonely and depressed. Not long after getting to San Francisco, I overdosed on alcohol and ended up in a coma. Polly got on a plane, came out to get me, then had me committed to a state hospital in Dayton.

When the other patients at the hospital found out I was a doctor, they got together one night and made fun of me, physically abused me, and finally ended up urinating on me. I remember lying there thinking, "This isn't making any sense." I said to myself, "If I ever get well, if I ever get out of this, I'm going to find a place for doctors to go to."

That was the germ of my dream.

I stayed at the state hospital for about three months. While I was there, a Roman Catholic priest, Father DeCavitt, came to see me and suggested that I try Alcoholics Anonymous. I'd love to say AA was magic, but it wasn't. I had trouble. I drank occasionally and still used some pills, but I kept going to meetings.

Father De Cavitt also sent me to see this doctor in Columbus, Dr. Charlie H. He was directing an alcohol treatment clinic at that time. He said I could work for him, but only if I did two things: I had to go to self-help meetings, and I had to travel around to alcoholism treatment centers and see what they were about. So I volunteered my services and visited almost every treatment center east of the Mississippi. Eventually I decided to give up internal medicine and cardiology, and go into addictionology. I spent two years training in addiction counseling, partly in Toronto, partly at Rutgers in New Brunswick, New Jersey.

In 1970, Senator Harold Hughes formed the National Institute of Alcohol and Alcohol Abuse. The first thing the institute did was heavily fund three cities—Philadelphia, Baltimore, and Seattle—to set up treatment centers for skid row bums. A lecturer at Rutgers said that the Maryland program needed a medical director and would I like the job? God, I hadn't had a paying job in three years, and I said I'd love it.

Shortly after I arrived in Baltimore, I realized that everything I'd read about skid row was malarkey and my studying had not prepared me for this new job. So I went to live with the skid row alcoholics and drug addicts. I panhandled, slept in the doorways of buildings and on the bridges, and got to know the folks. It was a marvelous experience—terribly frightening, terribly traumatic—but it was also a spiritual experience in some ways. After living on the street for three months, I came back out and ran that program as medical director for three years.

During this period, I was abstinent, but I was not sober; in other words, I was not drinking, I was going to meetings, but I was not living happily and productively in all aspects of my life, which is the true definition of sobriety.

At one point, Baltimore had a police strike. I heard from some of my friends on the street that some thugs were planning to raid my treatment center in order to get drugs. For three nights I sat up in the treatment center with a shotgun because there were no police around. After that, I was so tense that I went to a drugstore and bought some Sominex to help me go to sleep. Seventy-two hours after taking the Sominex I took a drink, my first in almost three years.

I didn't have more than an ounce of booze, but I knew I was in trouble. So I arranged to go to this marvelous treatment center called Chit Chat Farms in Pennsylvania. I spent twenty-nine days at Chit Chat Farms, and that's when my sobriety really started because that's when I began to accept alcoholism as a disease.

At the end of 1974, our grant ran out in Baltimore. I hadn't forgotten my dream to establish a treatment center for doctors, and I now was determined to go ahead. I talked to some folks at the Georgia State Medical Association and knew they were interested in forming some sort of treatment program for physicians. So I came down to Georgia in late 1974 and started a program formally in 1975. In 1977, I came out to Ridgeview.

Ridgeview was a psychiatric institute, but it had no alcohol or drug programs. There was one empty building and they agreed to let me use it for my own program with my own staff. I started from scratch, put my own staff together, started admitting patients, and launched the Impaired Professionals Program.

* * *

By mid-October, two facts had been well established. First, I was the sickest patient any of the staff or any of the other patients had ever seen, and they told me so often, usually when I was being reprimanded for some infringement. Second, for some reason, I had become Talbott's special pet.

The staff regarded my illness as extremely grave for numerous reasons: I was a polydrug addict, hooked on many different drugs; I had tried to commit suicide within hours of my arrival; I'd had a number of physical problems, including abscessed teeth and chronic malnutrition; my marriage to Paul was highly disturbed; and I was emotionally immature. My immaturity made life difficult for me and for everybody else. Although I was a doctor, I didn't look much like the other addicted or alcoholic doctors; I looked, and acted, like a troubled teenager. Most of the other patients I befriended were youths who had been put into an adult unit because they happened to be over the age of eighteen. Like me, however, they acted like twelve-year-olds.

I got into trouble all the time. I'd have trouble getting to groups on time. I'd wander off. I'd have temper tantrums about any and every little thing. I would deliberately break little rules, like playing hard rock ("druggie") music on my radio or refusing to make my bed or take a bath. If someone asked me to write an assignment, I would do anything I could to get out of doing it. Most of the rules I broke were minor ones, but the cumulative effect of continued and repeated pushing of limits was significant.

There were two very serious never-to-be-broken rules in treatment: Do not use drugs; and do not form intense personal relationships with other patients. I never used drugs, but I did form a couple of strong relationships, not sexual ones, but friendships deep enough to alarm the staff. One friend of mine, William, was gay. He would crawl in bed with me, and we would giggle like kindergarteners. This drove the staff crazy. Then a kid named Josh arrived in early October. He and I hit it off immediately, mostly because he had done dope much the same as I had. He had told everyone to get screwed, and then he just shoveled in the dope. I liked that in my men at that time.

We'd throw little spur-of-the-moment parties for ourselves. On one occasion, four or five of us ordered a pizza and then just started to celebrate. This was decidedly unacceptable to the staff. A few days before Halloween, the unit decided to throw a nice little recovery-oriented affair for the patients. But three of us decided to add our own twist to the festivities. We played hard rock music and wore unacceptable costumes. Josh painted his face white and wore a white sheet, pretending he was dead. I wrote "addict" in red paint across my forehead and painted "I'll die before I surrender" on a napkin I'd stolen from the dining room. I dripped red paint down my arm to look like the droplets of blood you get when you shoot up. In other words, we focused on drug-oriented jokes—only the staff didn't think they were so funny. The next day, they put us on restriction.

At the time that I came through treatment, few other patients exhibited my particular brand of pathology. Today, partly because drug use is beginning at an earlier age, the unit is full of people who look and act the way I did, but at the time I seemed different from the typical middle-aged professional alcoholic, and since my drug use had begun at an early age, I was noticeably sicker.

To my knowledge, no one has ever been kicked out of treatment at Ridgeview, but if a patient continually refuses to comply with the rules and does not respond to treatment due to his or her own obduracy, that patient may be transferred to another treatment facility. A general practitioner won't continue to treat a patient for high blood pressure if that patient refuses to take the prescribed pills, and the same is true with an addictionologist. A Ridgeview patient who continues to take drugs, has sexual relations, or is violent will probably be asked to go somewhere else. At Ridgeview, at least three recommendations are made, and often the staff makes all the arrangements for the transfer.

Early in my treatment, my disease was so malignant and my behavior was so rebellious that various members of the staff wanted to transfer me on numerous occasions. But Talbott defended me to the end.

G. Douglas Talbott: They used to kid me on the unit, especially when people wanted to throw her out. "There's Dr. Talbott's surrogate daughter getting all this special attention," they would say. And I'd reply, "You're right. Martha's very special to me, and you're not going to touch her."

Early on, some members of the staff felt that she wasn't responding. They wanted to send her up to a long-term treatment center in New Jersey called Alina Lodge. But I ran things around there. Polly says I'm very flexible as long as you do things my way. So I steamrolled Martha.

By the third week in October, I still felt hopeless, but I was still willing to try, even though by this time I'd been in Phase I (in-hospital treatment) longer than anyone had ever been. Most patients were released from Ridgeview after twenty-nine days, but my stay went on and on. Although I was frustrated with the slowness of my recovery and complained bitterly to Talbott, I knew he was right to keep me hospitalized. I still was not willing to commit myself to a lifetime of not taking drugs. Although I was not using, I did not yet have an honest desire to stop using. I was willing to stop dying, but that was the extent of my willingness.

I became obsessed with the words of the song "Snowblind," by Styx, and I was overcome with a craving for cocaine. I could see that I was totally "snowblind," incapacitated by the overwhelming, compulsive, irrational urge to use this drug.

Although I knew I would die if I used cocaine, I was equally convinced that I would die if I couldn't use it.

G. Douglas Talbott: Martha's treatment took longer than most because her disease was very malignant. Just like rheumatoid arthritis or tuberculosis that had gone untreated for fourteen or fifteen years, her disease was much more difficult to treat and took longer to heal. This disease was rampant in her for years. I don't think Martha would have lived three or four more years if she had gone on using drugs. In fact, I know she would have died. She'd gone as far as she could go with her disease and still live.

Toward the middle of October, the staff elected me community leader, which meant I was in charge of setting up meetings and assuming certain leadership roles. I almost lost what little emotional stability I had achieved because I felt the responsibility was too much for me at that time. Moreover, I felt that they were asking me to perform again. In fact, by assigning me this role, they were indicating that they were beginning to see some improvement. Despite their optimism, I sometimes believed that the staff let me stay in treatment only because I was such an excellent example of terminal end stage addiction and because I served as a deterrent to others.

Toward the end of October, I received indications from Talbott and some of the other staff members that my discharge to a halfway house was being considered. I couldn't believe it—and I was thrilled. At the same time, I began to get nervous. I'd heard from other patients about the stringent rules that were enforced in the halfway house system, and I'd heard stories about the director of the system, Donnie Brown.

Donnie was to the halfway house system what Talbott was to the Impaired Professionals Program—the last word. I'd seen Donnie at Ridgeview many times. He was a large man, about fifty years old, and looked like an ex–football player. Rumor had it that he could be highly confrontational and rigid; in other words, he was one tough dude who cleaned house for even the slightest infringement.

Donnie conducted the Saturday morning health professional therapy sessions. About a week before my discharge from Phase I, since he knew I would be transferring into the halfway house system within the next few days, he apparently decided to let me know who was in control. I was used to confrontation by this time, but I had never experienced anything like this.

At the Saturday therapy session, Donnie said to me, "Get away from that guy and move over there. I'm running this game. What makes you think you're ready to leave Ridgeview Institute? I'm scared for you. It makes me angry that the Ridgeview staff has messed up your treatment for more than six weeks and now I have to straighten things out. They've coddled you.

"You're too seductive. Guys, pull in your horns and leave her alone. That's the only way she'll get to know herself. I know all about you. You don't get along with your mother and you love your father. Do you really wonder why you went into psychiatry? You've been in a power struggle all your life. You're acting out all over the place—just like the adolescent you are. Who are you so angry at?"

I had sat through this tirade appearing totally controlled, and my reply was equally controlled: "Everyone. Myself, mostly. My parents, my husband, being here, and the disease."

"What are you scared of?" Donnie said.

He was really starting to piss me off, but it would have been a cold day in hell before I showed him my anger. I replied, as calmly as possible, "Leaving here and having no fucking control."

"Yeah, you're powerless, and you have no control," Donnie went on. "You need discipline. You're afraid of rejection. You need to get honest. The whole halfway house is in an uproar.

— 183 —

They're afraid of you. You need to do what you're told. Our treatment staff will expend the time and energy to help you. You'll get well, but I'm in control. You're not. Be honest and concentrate on recovery.

"You're afraid of women," he continued. "You need to learn to be with the women first, and then men. It scares me that you've had so much trouble here with control and you've needed so much structure. There are more rules in the halfway house than there are here, but there's less structure. You're meaner than hell. And now I've got to do Ridgeview's work so you don't blow up the entire halfway house system. I'm going to clean out your mouth, make a lady out of you, and teach you what discipline means."

My rage was so intense that I felt like killing him, and most of the other members of the group supported me; they told me afterward that they had never seen such an intense confrontation. One woman who had been present told me her theory of the halfway house system. She called it the "mushroom theory": They keep you in the dark and pile on the shit, and somehow you grow. I wasn't quite sure what she meant, but I was certain my association with Donnie Brown was going to be quite different from my relationship with Talbott. This was not a man who was going to come to my rescue if I screwed up. I was scared.

Donnie Brown: I remember Martha very well—I'd nailed her as soon as she finished withdrawal and started participating in hospital life. I saw her as a person with a lot of pathology—I never saw the cute side back then. She looked like she came off the street. Hyper. She watched hard and she learned fast. I knew that she'd had a long history with drugs. She'd been totally rebellious, and there was no structure to her life. She was running full and loose, and she was scared of that.

Her memories of this time, though, are a little different from mine. I led the health professionals therapy group for several years before Martha arrived, and I was there every Saturday, (at least) while she was in treatment, but she doesn't seem to remember me much until she was ready to go into the halfway house system. She seems to think I was scared of her. Hell, I wasn't scared of her, I was scared *for* her. Some people call me a real junkyard dog, but I care. I tell the truth, but I love these people. I may seem real strong, but it comes from caring and love. And I cared about Martha. But I was scared for her, too. She had a lot of growing to do.

During this same week, Paul came to Atlanta and we were subjected to an intense family workshop. I could see that I had no hope of salvaging our marriage; at the same time, I could not deal with the details of divorce. As a result, we decided to leave our problems on hold—a rather cold hold—until I was further along with my recovery. He brought me my car and gave me some money for clothes. I could see that he was in great pain, worried about me and anguished over the breakdown of our marriage.

Four days later, on October 30, I was discharged from Phase I of the Impaired Professionals Program and from Ridgeview Institute. The staff had kept me alive and had loved me unconditionally, no matter how hard I tried to push them away. They'd given me exactly what I needed—love and guidance—and forced me to take it. And Talbott had believed in me.

The following night I returned for the "graduation ceremony" and was given, as were all patients who completed treatment, a "12 & 12," a copy of the twelve steps and the twelve traditions of Alcoholics Anonymous.

Talbott wrote in mine, "May you know the third promise of AA." That promise reads: "We will comprehend the word serenity, all the torment and agony I'd endured just might have been worth it.

That night I wrote in my diary: "God, thanks for my life." It was still dark in my world, but for the first time I could see the hint of a ray of sunshine.

13
JOURNEY WITHOUT A DESTINATION

Immediately after being discharged from Ridgeview, I moved into a women's halfway house in Stone Mountain, Georgia, an Atlanta suburb about 40 miles east of Ridgeview. The normal tenure in a halfway house is three months, one month as part of Phase II (outpatient treatment), and two months as part of Phase III (professional placement). Since my stay in Phase I had been approximately twice as long as a normal hospital stay, I suspected I would be equally slow to adjust to the remaining two phases of the program—and I was right. I lived in the halfway house system for more than six months.

At the time, Phase II of the Impaired Professionals Program was connected with an organization called DAC (DeKalb Addiction Clinic), which was an intensive outpatient drug treatment program working in conjunction with Ridgeview, the Impaired Professionals Program, and various halfway house systems. Outpatient treatment allowed the patient to slowly get used to day-to-day living outside the hospital before he or she returned to the stresses of work. We'd go to the DAC center at 8:30 or 9:00 in the morning, attend various group therapy sessions and lectures until about 3:00, then return to the halfway house, often for a "house" therapy session. In the evening, we'd catch a quick dinner, then go to yet another self-help support meeting. At the end of the day, I would usually jog, then write or read for a few hours, then go to bed. I was still not able to sleep soundly and would finally nod off about two or three, then sleep only until six.

Donnie Brown: I had been the director of MARR, Metro Atlanta Recovery Residences, for several years by the time I met Martha, and had worked closely with Ridgeview and DAC, the DeKalb Addiction Clinic, which ran the outpatient programs. In addition to managing MARR, I lectured and conducted groups at Ridgeview and DAC. With MARR, DAC, and Ridgeview, each director had equal authority; we worked in tandem.

When a patient moves into the halfway house, he or she is required to share a house or apartment with five or six other people, all of the same sex, some of whom are medical professionals, some not. No staff member is present in the living situation, although we have a set of rules with the expectation that, by the time the patient enters the halfway house, he is responsible. It is based on the family model, and new members are taken in, much the way you'd take in a new baby or child. How each person responds is a reflection of his or her health. But we run it the way they ran the troops in *The Dirty Dozen*—very confrontationally.

We are very clear about rules. No using, of course. Emotional or physical pairing off is forbidden. No pets; no guns or knives. We insist on strict curfews: 10:00 on weeknights, 1:30 on Friday and Saturday, 11:30 on Sunday. We watch for any behavior that reflects a lazy attitude, and we confront that. And you can't miss a group therapy session.

In the halfway house, we have three therapy sessions each week, on Mondays, Wednesdays, and Thursdays. (These sessions are in addition to therapy sessions at DAC.) The sessions are conducted in the halfway house itself; in other words, instead of going to a doctor's office, you stay home. Again, it's like a family. You can't escape.

In MARR, we also insist that patients attend a spiritual life group each week. We send staff members out into the religious community and they train a pastor to deal with the problems of a recovering addict. We have a full range of spiritual life groups—Protestant, Catholic, Jewish—and we feel that the spiritual work is as important to recovery as the physical and psychological work.

One of the people most crucial to me, and most confrontational toward me, throughout my months in the halfway house was Donnie Brown. As he—and I—had feared, I had tremendous problems abiding by the rules of DAC and of MARR, Donnie Brown's halfway house system; but unlike Talbott, Donnie was not a coddling, oversensitive individual, at least not overtly. He could seem harsh and highly confrontational, but since he is a deeply religious man, he does this out of love and caring for the addict. At the time, however, I couldn't see this. I also suspected that from the start, Donnie was after me because I was Talbott's pet. He and Talbott had disagreed in the past over the substance and style of drug treatment, so in a sense I felt like I got caught in the crossfire.

Donnie Brown: Apparently Martha was deeply affected by the split between Doug Talbott and me, but I never felt that my feelings for her were part of that. It is true that Doug and I disagreed on a number of issues. (We parted company in 1983 or so.) I felt from the beginning of the Impaired Professionals Program that I was a key person in its development and that MARR was important to its success. I even won the Caduceus award one year.

Toward the end, Doug and I were like meter rats running together. He wanted more control, but I felt we should share control to keep it balanced. Also, sometimes I was tougher than Talbott. One time, a group of four or five doctors, men and women patients in the halfway house, staged a pizza party after an AA meeting. This went against the rules, and I insisted that they leave—all of them. I arranged other housing, but this was a clear violation and they all knew it. This sort of thing was very hard on Talbott.

With two personalities as strong as Doug's and mine, each of us seeing things in opposite ways, our parting was inevitable. But, for me, our breaking apart was like a very painful divorce.

Ultimately, Donnie taught me discipline, and as a result, I survived. Many times he shouted at me: "You sick bitch. You sick bitch." But because I had no other place to go (and because I *was* a sick bitch), I put up with it. I was not compliant, however. I broke every rule and tested every limit. He endured my rebelliousness most of the time, and when he did run out of patience, Talbott stepped in to rescue me.

In addition to my repeated confrontations with Donnie, my biggest problem in the halfway house was living with women. I had been told repeatedly during Phase I that I had to "get with the women," that I had to learn to relate to women better before I could maintain a healthy relationship with a man. I could think of few activities as distasteful to me as "getting with the women," mostly because I thought I related better to men, but in the halfway house I had no choice.

My problems with women had to do with issues of control and manipulation. All my life, I'd been able to manipulate men, starting with my dad and my brother. Throughout my therapy in the hospital and later as an outpatient, I was reprimanded often for being seductive and manipulative. The staff told me that I might be good at getting what I wanted from men, but I sure as hell was not good at getting what I needed. I would learn what I needed—how to trust people, for example—only through intimate relationships with women.

Over the next six months, I lived with nine different women all together, since patients were constantly being transferred in and out of the halfway house. I was the only physician in the group, but all of us had our drug problems—and our femininity—in common. Through each of my roommates I learned something different. These women served as mirrors for me. In them I could see my disease and how it manifested itself. I also saw in them an array of problems and feelings that I'd experienced all my life but never truly shared, even with close friends like Maggie and Connie. I had had many mixed feelings—mostly negative—about my mother, and I came to see that those feelings affected my response not only to most other women but to myself. I didn't become lifelong friends with any of the women I lived with, but they taught me plenty and guided me through a crucial growing process.

Donnie Brown: From the beginning it was obvious that Martha never got on with women. She avoided them every way she could—and there were always enough guys around for her to avoid relating to the other women. In general, it's always easier for men to get together than women. In a way, women are more competitive with each other. For whatever reason, they have faster mood swings and greater shame and guilt than men do—or at least they seem to be able to get at those feelings faster. I suspect these were some of the reasons relationships with women were scary to Martha.

Before leaving Phase I, I had been required to set out the goals I intended to achieve during Phase II and afterward. These were mine:

1. Stay straight and sober.
2. Resolve marital and familial conflict.
3. Learn to relate with females and with males to improve interpersonal relations.

4. Improve physical health and nutritional status.
5. Learn about addiction and disease concept.

GROWTH GOALS

1. Learn how to express anger appropriately.
2. Deal with chronic loneliness.
3. Enhance spirituality.
4. Resolve control issues and increase responsibility.
5. Stop intellectualizing.
6. Learn moderation.

Despite all these good, self-righteous intentions, the moment I walked out the door of Ridgeview Institute, I broke the second most important rule in treatment: I had an affair. I had been told repeatedly—from the moment Tom and Jack picked me up at the airport—that relationships were dangerous early in recovery. What's more, since I was about to be hit with a divorce suit from Paul, an affair could complicate my life legally and possibly cause severe repercussions.

But, of course, I was different. "They" didn't understand this relationship. My situation was unique.

Dylan was a cardiologist whom I met at a meeting of the International Doctors in AA. He was himself recovering, having been through the Impaired Professionals Program a few years before. He was four years older than I, very successful and married. He and his wife were having marital difficulties and were seeing Donnie Brown for counseling. Donnie didn't take private patients often, but he was particularly fond of Dylan. Characteristically, I plunged in, asking for trouble. I stepped into Donnie's halfway house and immediately got involved with one of his prize patients, the very person who was to Donnie what I was to Talbott. I could not have taken a more self-destructive step.

Nothing very serious developed for several weeks. The day I was discharged from Ridgeview, I met Dylan for coffee. We sat around and chatted, realizing that we shared a number of interests. Like me, for example, he seemed to be stuck in the eighteen- or nineteen-year-old age bracket, and he still had a great love for rock music. For the next month, we met a couple of times a week, just to talk.

By early December, however, the relationship had begun to heat up. Nevertheless, I thought that if we were not sleeping together, it was all okay. I even announced at a Caduceus meeting that I had fallen in love with a special man, but was not sleeping with him, and therefore was handling it well. No one believed me.

Two weeks before Christmas, I was granted my first independent seventy-two-hour TL (therapeutic leave). Dylan and I spent the first night of my leave at the Airport Marriott Hotel. Then I flew to Little Rock and stayed one night with Maggie and Mac, followed by one night in Fayetteville with my parents.

My one night with Dylan was all very romantic and exciting. I was euphoric, in love, finally free to spend a couple of days with my friends and family. To my mind, things were coming together. I was finally on a leave—my first in almost four months. I had been feeling sorry for myself because I was the only one of the group I entered treatment with who was still in treatment. I would be in the placement phase for at least two more months and probably longer. And it was Christmastime.

All of my attitudes and actions were classic behavior for a sick, still-recovering addict, but I didn't realize that at the time. After my visit to Little Rock, Maggie sent a letter to Talbott assuring him that she had taken good care of me. Her tone reflects my own great spirits:

December 1981
To whom it may concern:

Martha Morrison has been in my constant care

and under my supervision for the past 3 ¼ days. During that time, she made no searches of my premises, consumed no chemicals, and much to my husband's chagrin, kept her hands to herself.

We would therefore highly recommend a repeat visit of longer duration.

> *Sincerely,*
> *Maggie*
> *Keeper of the Impaired Physician*

When I returned to Atlanta, Dylan and I started seeing each other frequently. This was the beginning of the end—or an end—for me, but I rushed in not knowing that within a few weeks I would be thrown back to the depths of despair.

But my feelings for Dylan were not the only emotions growing during this period. By this time, I was well aware that I had extreme difficulty expressing my feelings. Until I entered treatment, I suspect I didn't even know what my feelings were most of the time. Then, as I gradually became able to identify a few emotions, I certainly had no idea how to express them appropriately. They were all so incredibly intense that I simply had no means by which to cope with them.

My greatest flaw was my attitude of "terminal uniqueness" coupled with my inability to reach out to others and ask for help. I was too sick, too different, too special, too everything. I was repeatedly confronted about this throughout treatment, but it proved to be a difficult and complex personality trait to grapple with because it stemmed from both a sense of grandiosity and a lack of self-worth.

I was also criticized repeatedly about my unwillingness or inability to give up trying to control and manipulate every person and situation I came in contact with. And I was taken to task for a related quality—my anger. Many times, my progress or lack of progress was so severely questioned (as it had been during inpatient treatment) that some of the staff threatened to kick me out of the program. Thank God, each time this happened, Talbott rescued me.

I had the distinct honor of being awarded the infamous WAIT (Worst Addict in Treatment) award. Other titles I earned in treatment were: Dr. Intensity, Low Profile, Dr. Organicity, Little Virgin Girl Doctor, Crisis Queen, Dr. Excitement, Talbott's Protégé, Pig Pen, Terminal End Stage Addict, Official Program Balls Bearer, Crazy Computer, Master Manipulator, Golden Girl, and the Ridgeview Miracle.

Yet despite days of confusion and discouragement, I began to learn about gratitude. In mid-December, shortly after my leave, I wrote a gratitude list that indicated that I was growing—at least a bit:

I'm grateful that

1. I'm straight and sober.
2. I'm alive.
3. I found Ridgeview and even DAC and the halfway house.
4. I'm changing.
5. I have an occasional calm moment when there was never peace before.
6. I don't always want to kill myself.
7. I'm beginning to love others.
8. I can let go of some of my guilt.
9. I am now human.
10. My parents love me.
11. I have friends at Ridgeview and in the halfway house who love me.
12. Maggie and Connie are wonderful friends.
13. I can feel.
14. I have a place to live.
15. I don't have to go home now.
16. My grandmother was alive and loved me as a kid.
17. I can fish.

18. I've had so many experiences.
19. That I am trying to recover from addiction.
20. I was hospitalized when I was seventeen.
21. I am trying to learn to be honest and trust others.
22. I have helped others.
23. I am getting closer to God.
24. I have the capacity to be grateful.

With the help of many people, with the grace of God, with loads of patience and time, I began to learn a little about recovery. Little did I know that by not using drugs, by attending meetings, and by trying to work my way through the steps of recovery I would ensure that all these things would be given to me—things like love, acceptance, freedom, security, hope, and peace of mind.

In January 1982, I was moved on to Phase III, the step known as "placement." During this phase (usually a period of two months), recovering doctors are placed in various alcohol and drug treatment settings under close supervision. In placement, they treat others who are in earlier stages of addiction. This is called "mirror imaging" and provides recovering doctors with a situation where they are able to see their disease clearly in someone else. I began placement at Peachtree Parkwood hospital and remained there for eight weeks.

By early January, my affair with Dylan was going full tilt. We were seeing each other almost every day, and I began lying to my roommates about where I was going and who I was seeing.

Dylan would show up at Peachtree Parkwood frequently. Nobody knew him, so we could sit openly in the cafeteria. Often we'd go over to his house when his wife was out of town. Other times, we'd meet at a friend's house or go to a motel for an afternoon. Within a month, however, the secrecy and the intensity of this affair were driving me nuts.

As I began to withdraw from him, Dylan grew more and more demanding and possessive. He'd show up at Peachtree

Parkwood after I'd told him not to come. He'd call me at Ridgeview when I was there for a meeting, and he'd come into the lobby of the halfway house and want me to come down—*now*. He'd pressure me to go to this motel or that hotel. He'd say this was the only afternoon he could get off, so I had to come.

He'd call me constantly at the halfway house. I told him to stop because I feared the staff would find out about us, but he kept calling anyway. I started to notice a wild-eyed look in his eyes that seemed to say, "You're mine, and nobody's going to separate us." It was as though he was addicted to me—and he was. I had gotten over my addiction to him, but his lingered and it really frightened me. This was the danger they'd all been warning me about. Relationships could be like dope— addictive, uncontrollable, and frightening. When I finally realized how crazy it was—and I was—I became suicidal.

I didn't know what to do or where to turn. I knew that if I confessed, they'd throw me out of treatment. I'd mentioned my "non-sexual" relationship in the Caduceus meeting, and the other docs were already sure I was lying. I knew Donnie would throw me out of the halfway house if he found out about Dylan. I knew if I got kicked out now, I would use and I would die. I had nowhere to go. I had no money. I was in the middle of a messy divorce. I was absolutely crazy with fear.

I had formed a friendship with another impaired physician, Beau Anderson, one of the few doctors who I felt really understood my pain. I decided to open up to Beau, and he insisted that I talk to Talbott.

Confessing to Talbott was like telling my father. I felt like a five-year-old. But he came to my defense immediately and had Dylan barred from Ridgeview for his good and for mine.

Nevertheless, Talbott forced me to take the entire issue before the Caduceus group. At that point, the group consisted of about fifty doctors, forty-nine of them men. I had to go down and tell these guys that I was having an affair with another doctor, that it was making me crazy and suicidal, and that I wanted to get out of it.

I knew their first impulse would be to kick me out, to send me away because it was the fourteen-millionth time I'd been in trouble. In fact, most of them did think I should leave. Then Talbott, who sat next to me during the whole "confession," turned the group around. They all took pity on me. They understood my vulnerability at this stage of recovery, and gave me one more chance, but not before I had to go around the room and be hugged by each and every one of them. I felt terribly ashamed and embarrassed.

But this wasn't the end of it. Once Donnie got wind of this major transgression, he was hell-bent on kicking me out. After all, I had blatantly violated one of the most important rules. All along, I'd felt that Donnie wanted me to keep getting into trouble because that would prove Talbott wrong. Whenever I came close to messing up I'd think, "Donnie will be right. I can't let that happen." That thought kept me clean—not sober, but clean. At times, too, Donnie could be even more overbearing than Talbott. This was precisely the sort of incident with potential for explosion, and Donnie and Talbott locked horns over it.

G. Douglas Talbott: This guy who was running our halfway houses at that time—Donnie Brown—was determined to throw Martha out. He said, "We'll have to get rid of her." And I said, "Over my dead body you'll get rid of her. If she leaves your organization, I'll form another organization, and I'll put her someplace else. But you're not going to throw her out."

Several times, different people wanted to get rid of Martha, but I saw a lot of things in her that impressed me. At that time I was preparing to start an adolescent program, and I saw her as a person who would be excellent doing that. Initially, when I talked about it, everyone had a fit! But I related to Martha in many ways. I could see a lot of potential in her. I thought she could be brought along quickly, and I figured she could be very useful.

Donnie Brown: For me, emotional pairing off is a major violation—the sexual issue is an addictive issue. We feel that during treatment and the halfway house experience, patients should focus only on their chemical addiction. Again, my memory of Martha's relationship with Dylan is a little different. I saw a lot of couples privately for marital therapy. I liked Dylan, but I don't recall that I was that close with him. Of course, I couldn't support an affair and I'm strong with everybody, but, as I remember, she was almost done with treatment when this happened so I don't think I wanted her to leave.

I felt that Talbott was co-dependent on Martha. It was obvious that she was special to him from the word go. At first I thought, "Who could care about this junkie?" I confronted him with this. It seemed to me that the more pathology patients brought to the situation, the more he personally advocated their cause. The other patients accepted Talbott's special favorites, but management and staff gave him more trouble.

I don't believe that Martha was as bad as she thinks that she was. She was scared to death.

The Caduceus incident marked the end of my affair with Dylan. A short time later, he and his wife separated and ultimately he relapsed. Finally, he went through treatment again, and today he's a successful doctor in Georgia.

Most physicians in the Ridgeview program served only one placement in Phase III of their treatment, but I was once again the slow learner: I had to serve three separate placements. I had served two months in placement already, the normal time, but when those two months ended in late February, I was given my second placement. This involved assisting at Smyrna General Hospital and performing additional duties at Georgia Alcohol and Drug Associates (GADA), a corporation of doctors directed by Doug Talbott.

Around that time I wrote, "I'm sick of this disease. I want out. I don't know if I can get well. I'm very tired of thinking about putting a needle in my arm every waking moment of every day." But, as much as I wanted to be free of my disease, I seemed incapable of exemplary behavior. Sometime in February my relationship with Beau Anderson became more than just a friendship.

Beau was a surgeon from Washington State who was about ten years older than I. He had done a lot of drugs, especially speed. Beau was about six months ahead of me in treatment and we had met at the Caduceus group. He was one of the first people I could relate to because I knew he had been as sick as I'd been. He was just far enough ahead of me to have a sharp understanding of what I was going through, yet assure me that things would get better.

At this time I still had symptoms of organic brain damage—in other words, I couldn't think straight. These symptoms had been acute during withdrawal, and they lingered for months afterward. I'd forget what I was saying in the middle of a sentence. I'd walk from one room to another and forget why I'd gone there or where I was. This would also happen while I was driving and I'd have to pull off the interstate. When this first happened, I got totally hysterical. It was Beau who made me believe that these episodes would pass. He advised me to stop, try to relax, and wait for the thought to come back to me.

I also had some severe panic attacks during this period. Beau had been through the same experience, and he assured me that I would get over them. He understood my problems when others in the program didn't have the vaguest idea what I was talking about.

For a while, Beau and I had great times together. We'd go up to the local Denny's and sit for hours getting wired on coffee and cigarettes. We'd cut up and act like degenerates, but we thought it was funny because we knew we were doctors even though we looked like hippies. We'd talk together about how much better we were than the other docs because we had been so much sicker. Then we'd drive all over Atlanta and get lost together, but we loved it. We'd be going someplace, and then we'd both kind of flake out and realize we had no idea where we were, but we had fun anyway.

I tried to keep my relationship with Beau a secret, but my roommates figured it out and began to come down on me—about Beau and about men in general. It began to appear to me that I was getting better, and slowly it became clear that I was as well as Beau, but had no hope of becoming truly well if I continued in the relationship.

Donnie Brown: I was also aware of her relationship with Beau Anderson. Beau was a needy person, and he liked to take care of her, protect her, mother her, just in order to be with her. I think Martha used him as just a companion, and they played with that. I never thought it was particularly serious. They were just two healthy pups getting together.

The more I began to appreciate the addictiveness of our relationship and the extent of my dependency on Beau, the more depressed I got. Once again I was running at full speed with my work and with my personal life, and I felt trapped. I'd been drug-free for six months, and I was supposed to feel that the sun was shining, but all I could see was black. I constantly felt the urge to use. I didn't know which was worse, the last six months of my active addiction or the first six months of my recovery. I was having problems with the whole program of recovery—I could not intellectually grasp the concept: I was still not ready to give up drugs completely, and I could not give up my control and "surrender" to God.

On March 24, 1982, I left Ridgeview—by then I was working at my *third* placement—feeling doomed, agonized, and hopeless. I went to a trail along the Chattahoochee River where I frequently hiked. It was pouring rain, but I didn't care. My time was up, and I knew it. I began hiking along the trail that snaked along the edge of the bluffs above the rapids. I was soaking wet from the rain, with just enough energy left to jump off the bluffs and into the rocks and rapids.

I knelt on the ground, tears streaming down my face. I screamed that simple prayer: "God, help me. I give up. Please let me die or let me get better."

Suddenly, I felt as if the weight of the world had been lifted from my shoulders. At first, I figured I had finally become irreversibly psychotic; this experience was too incredible. The warmth, the peace of mind, the profound sense of relief, just washed over me. Just as suddenly, the rain let up and, as corny as it sounds, a rainbow appeared over the waters of the Chattahoochee. That all-powerful, overwhelming urge to use drugs had been lifted from me, and I knew a freedom I had never known before.

I knew beyond doubt that God had heard me. He had answered my prayer for help. Without quite realizing it, I had surrendered to Him, and that surrender had brought me hope and serenity. I finally found the "God of my understanding," and I was no longer alone.

Ironically, as I walked away from the riverbank, I met two young men smoking pot. They offered me a joint, but I refused, knowing I could not have done that fifteen minutes earlier. The compulsion to use drugs—the compulsion I had lived with all my life—was really gone. I knew a truly wonderful freedom and a new happiness.

I believe this was a true spiritual awakening. I admitted my powerlessness and finally became so exhausted that I had absolutely nowhere to turn, so I turned to God out of desperation. As a result, I came to understand the first hurdle of recovery: I was powerless over the disease and my life was totally unmanageable. I finally came to believe that I, too, could get better because I accepted and understood that there was a power greater than myself that could and would take care of me. I knew I would recover with God's help—and the help of others. I realized that my will and my way would not work, but that God's will and God's way would, if I surrendered to Him.

The foundation was finally in place.

Donnie Brown: I remember the incident on the Chattahoochee. I was seeing her privately a couple of times a week at that time, and she had started coming to my church. One Sunday, we had an altar call at church, and Martha went forward and confessed publicly her need for God. She was struggling with her moral conscience, and in our church we stress the importance and reality of an individual's higher and lower nature. We believe each person has the freedom to choose his or her higher or lower self. One of the things I helped her do was to get in touch with her better nature.

As a result of my spiritual awakening, I had the strength to actively and rationally deal with the problems in my life. For starters, I broke off with Beau. When we'd started our relationship, he'd been a friend who kept saying, "Don't run, don't use, and survive." Other than Talbott, he was the only person I trusted completely. But when Beau and I became closer, my addictive tendencies were activated. We fed into each other's sickness, we became too dependent on each other, we became each other's fix. Then, it seemed to me, I had surpassed him in recovery, if only in that I understood what was happening with regard to our relationship. It was precisely the danger—again—that I'd been warned about since the beginning of treatment: Next to drugs, relationships were the most addictive thing going.

The breakup was traumatic for both of us, but I did it—not with the crazy panic I'd experienced when my affair with Dylan got out of hand, but with a sense of responsibility. Sadly, after our final break Beau and I didn't speak for a long, long time. His pain was profound, and so was mine. But things were looking up. I had started to get better. Today, Beau is sober, successful, and a very dear and close friend.

In April, I moved into what is called a three-quarter way house, a living situation designed for people like me who have completed the halfway house phase of treatment but have no other place to go. (During this phase, therapy is also reduced to once-a-week sessions.) Most people who come into treatment return to their home, their spouse, their parents, whatever. I had no permanent job, no permanent home, and was in the process of divorce. To return to Arkansas, to my residency and the pressures of my divorce, would have been overwhelming. I was getting better, but I was still too fragile to cope with so intensive a crisis.

When I'd gone into the halfway house, Paul had given me a car and some money, and my uncle had allowed me to borrow $5,000 from his bank in Little Rock. But by April, those funds had run out, I had to go on a vocational rehabilitation welfare program, which provided just enough money to pay rent, car expenses, and food. Normally, of course, doctors were not considered candidates for welfare, but I got friendly with a man at the vocational rehab center who agreed to remove the "M.D." from my application, so I got the welfare payments. As it turned out, this man was an active alcoholic. Later, after I was sober and working, he came out to Ridgeview to hear me give a workshop. As a result, he went back into AA and is now sober. It was a nice exchange of gifts.

I had grown a lot in the months of my halfway house experience, yet I carried a few grudges, particularly toward Donnie, who for the entire six months had been relentless in his criticism of me and my behavior. But I was learning that to carry grudges means to be angry, miserable, and perhaps ultimately drunk—and I couldn't afford that. For me, using meant dying. I learned that I had to find the good side, the positive aspect, of any situation.

Donnie had taught me things that made a profound difference in my recovery—little pearls that I remember often and which affect the way I live. He used to say, "God doesn't shut one door that he doesn't open a window." Well, God had slammed a lot of doors in my face all through treatment and early recovery, but always God had opened a window, too. Donnie also used to say, "It is through our weaknesses that God's strength is made known." My weakness was chemical dependency, and it was through that weakness that I came to know myself, my strengths, and my God.

It's curious, but Donnie was responsible for getting me involved in the church, which particularly pleased my parents. He taught me discipline. And he taught me faith. And I grew to love him.

Donnie Brown: I believe I was one of the key people in Martha's recovery. I was with her, I was available, and I was honest. Truth without love is harsh, but if you care about someone, truth is healing. I cared about her, and she grew. It wasn't easy, but she did. Her parents are fine people. I always told her she had a heritage to uphold. Martha is a tender and special woman—especially in her work now with teenagers, but also as a human being.

* * *

I was finally discharged from the Impaired Professionals Program in May 1982, almost nine months after I'd entered what was supposed to have been a four-month program. On May 23, I became formally employed by GADA and began work at Ridgeview. In June 1982, my divorce was final, marking the end of my long, anguish-riddled relationship with Paul. In July 1982, I moved out of the three-quarter-way house into my very own apartment overlooking the Chattahoochee River.

14
BLOOD, SWEAT, AND GOLDEN OPPORTUNITIES

Most of us have seen death close up.
We have known the kind of suffering that wrenches the bones.
But we have also known the sort of hope that makes the heart sing.
LIVING SOBER

Once I realized that I would probably live through treatment, I knew I had to work in the field of alcoholism and drug treatment. In retrospect, I'd always known that drugs were the most significant factor in my life and that I would probably eventually work in the field. This insight had caused me considerable conflict, particularly during the last couple of years before I entered treatment, because my own intake had increased in direct proportion to my work with abusers and addicts. It finally became impossible for me to rationalize the contradiction.

In May 1982, after nine months of treatment, I found myself discharged but without a job and with no means of support. I sent a long and loving letter to Dr. Randall explaining why I would not be returning to Arkansas. I suppose Dr. Randall thought I was crazy—and quite frankly, I still was—but I did make the correct decision.

Fortunately, I was offered two very good jobs—one was a chance to launch an adolescent drug treatment unit at a fine private psychiatric hospital outside Knoxville, Tennessee; the other was an opportunity to become the first recovering doctor to run a chemically dependent adolescent unit at the Psychiatric Institute of Richmond, Virginia. Both seemed like good offers, particularly as they did not require that I have any additional training.

However, Dr. Talbott also offered me a position with the Georgia Alcohol and Drug Association (GADA) as an associate doctor, and that was the offer I finally accepted. He arranged for me to complete my medical training through Emory University, which helped me to finish my general psychiatry residency. He also offered me a fellowship in conjunction with Ridgeview and Emory, the first addictionology fellowship in the United States. Ridgeview and the Impaired Professionals Program offered the best drug treatment facility in America, and Dr. Talbott was one of the leading addictionologists in the United States, so it only seemed logical that this is where I should complete my training.

G. Douglas Talbott: I wanted to keep Martha here at Ridgeview at that point to run my adolescent unit, so I went down to Emory and talked to them about having her go back into training. I had had problems getting back into academic medicine after my recovery because I was not a psychiatrist, and psychiatry is where drug and alcohol addiction is treated. I talked to quite a lot of people down at Emory. We started a fellowship which we awarded to Martha, and then we got her accepted to Emory.

Of course, it was extremely difficult for me to separate myself from Arkansas. Until I came into treatment, my whole life had been in Arkansas—my friends, my family, my roots. But I was newly divorced, newly sober, and ready to begin a new life.

On the day after I was discharged, after having been in

treatment for nine months with essentially no income, I went to work as a consultant at GADA for $500 a month. This was a small salary, even compared to a resident's salary, but it was all I needed. Too much money would have been very dangerous for me.

In June 1982, I had another spiritual experience. Once again, I had been struggling with control issues, feeling different from others, and allowing my priorities to get out of balance. At this time, I was working at Ridgeview, treating adults with chemical dependence and working closely with the IPP, not as a patient but as a doctor. I fell back into the trap of needing to look good and perform well instead of just being me. I became overwhelmed.

On June 26, I left Atlanta and went to the North Georgia mountains to camp and hike. Many of my friends thought I was crazy to go way off in the mountains alone, which I did fairly frequently, but I felt safe there. I would hike 15 or 20 miles, burn off excess energy, clear my mind, cry, write, talk to God, and read.

On this particular day, I was hiking near an old dirt road when I came upon a little white church out in the middle of nowhere. I went in and stood at the altar and talked openly to God, trying to clarify to Him and to myself the emotions and fears I was experiencing. Then I knelt and began to pray. I didn't know if I was going to be able to continue on the path of recovery because I felt so weighted down, as if I would never be able to get up and carry the load I was being asked to carry.

Incredibly, relief washed over me. I felt as if God had said to me, "Stand up. Rise and go forth." Once again, in my time of weakness, I was able to find God's strength. I felt that God was trying to tell me to slow down and listen. Over the next few months, I had a few other less dramatic experiences that I felt allowed me to let go and let God share my load. It takes a lot to get my attention, I guess.

By August 1982, I had obtained full medical privileges at Ridgeview and had become an official member of GADA. On November 1, 1982, barely one year sober, I began my last year of psych residency at Emory and concurrently began a year of formal addictionology training. By this time, I had already begun to travel with Talbott, attending and speaking at national AA conferences, addiction workshops, and psychiatric conferences. In autumn 1983, I completed my psych and addictionology requirements and training.

Before I could obtain hospital privileges and licensing, I was placed under a consent order by the Georgia Medical Board of Examiners. This order was instituted in October 1982 and lasted for two years, during which my practice of medicine was restricted and closely supervised and I had to surrender my narcotic and DEA license. At the time, I was furious that I had to comply with this law (I could have returned to Arkansas with a totally unrestricted license), but I later realized it was exactly what I needed—another lesson in acceptance. I ended up being very grateful that I could practice at all.

On September 11,1982, I celebrated my first year of sobriety. Astonishingly, I had not used drugs or alcohol for 365 days. No other experience was more profound or important to me than this one. It was even as spiritual as the two major awakenings I'd had while hiking.

On my first sobriety birthday I was "high" all day. That night my friends and co-workers threw a party for me at a local recovery clubhouse. I was surprised that I had made it, and so were a lot of other people. I felt intense gratitude to all my new friends who had shown me the way, accepted me unconditionally, and cared about me when I didn't care about myself or them. I have never known a more loving and accepting group of people. I saw recovery as I'd never seen it before; I saw blessings and God's grace. It was truly nothing short of a miracle.

By this time I'd been working at GADA and Ridgeview for

about four months, and Talbott and I had begun to become friends. We were a lot alike, right down to a certain craziness. He would constantly joke with me, after I began to get well, about my having been the sickest of the sick. I would return with a retort about how hopelessly incurable he was. He was the first person I'd ever met who could keep up with and in some ways surpass my level of energy.

Because of the example he had set, I began to see the value of keeping the door to my past open. I began to see how my experiences could benefit others, as the story of his life had benefited me. I began to realize that no matter how far down I had gone, my experience could be useful to others.

We began to travel together to speak at other treatment centers and at universities and national conferences. At first, I just rode along and listened and met other professionals in the field. Then I began speaking, too. I enjoyed lecturing, and I was good at it, because I had a message. I knew exactly what the patients were going through. I understood the denial, the devastated families, and the shame and guilt of alcoholism and drug addiction. Because of my treatment and recovery, I knew what they needed in order to get well.

G. Douglas Talbott: Martha bummed around with me. I wanted her to see trust and closeness, and to relate to people who could relate to one another, yet give each other space and time. I introduced her to my children in the hope that she might see that kind of interrelationship in my family.

Once again, however, I met resistance from some of my associates at Ridgeview. They resented my "favorite daughter" position and felt I was allowed to go public with my story too soon. At the same time, I was forming a number of close friendships with other doctors that I worked with. Among them were Art Carpenter and Philip Wilson, who remain two of my closest friends. Art is now associated with another hospital, but Philip and I work together to this day. He is a specialist in internal medicine. Although he is not a recovering addict, he has a long family history of alcoholism.

Philip Wilson: When I met Doug, I was working at a public alcohol and drug treatment center in downtown Atlanta. One day I admitted this old fellow who told me he was a pharmacist. I said, "Right." The next day he told me he was also a doctor, and I said: "Sure you are . . . and I'm the pope." But lo and behold, this addict *was* a doctor and a pharmacist.

He was just the sweetest old man. I had heard that this fellow here in Georgia had started a program for impaired physicians, so we contacted this guy by the name of Doug Talbott, who rushed over and saw this fellow in my treatment center and took him away. Talbott then asked me if I'd be interested in helping out in his program, and I accepted.

The first I heard of Martha was when she was admitted to Cottage A. It was pretty hard not to hear about her. She was loud-mouthed, obstreperous, denying. She made a ruckus. She was very anxious, very skittish, scared. I guess she was feeling trapped. She was frightened and was acting out her feelings. We really didn't get to know each other for some time, but I knew Martha was around.

Obviously she is very aggressive and compulsive. That always helps. Doug stuck by her; she was his *cause célèbre*. Other people would say, "She is like the favorite child. She's getting all these special favors." I think Doug saw a lot of himself in Martha. Here was someone who was really sick, suicidal, who had lost everything. Hopeless. Helpless. To see someone come back from the depths of despair and depression is really something. There is no way you can pass that up.

In early 1983, I began to coordinate one of the adult chemical dependence units, and I started teaching substance abuse classes to Emory medical students. Meanwhile, I was speaking publicly, attending a lot of conferences, and attempting to learn as much as I could from as many different people as possible. The next two years, 1983 and 1984, were very busy ones professionally. I began to be invited to major addiction conferences, including those sponsored by the America Medical Association, the American Psychiatric Association, the American Psychological Association, and the National Association for Alcoholism and Drug Abuse Counselors. I also received a fair amount of media exposure, including a feature on ABC's *Nightline*, an appearance on CBS News *Sunday Morning*, and a story in *Newsweek*.

In October 1983, Talbott had me appointed associate director of the adolescent chemical dependence unit at Ridgeview. Prior to this, GADA's services had been limited to adults and health professionals, but it was now imperative that we address the burgeoning adolescent drug problem. Two years before, I had planned to begin an adolescent psych fellowship in Arkansas, but I had entered treatment instead. Now I was offered that chance again. Unlike most other addictionologists, I loved working with kids, particularly adolescents. I could relate to them, and they, generally, to me. I knew what they were going through and what they needed in order to come out on the other side. I also felt that as an adolescent I had been misdiagnosed and incorrectly treated. I still wanted to change the world, and more than anything, I wanted to carry my message of hope and recovery to as many people as possible. Where better to start than with teenagers? These were the kids who would one day change the world.

G. Douglas Talbott: I'd had Martha in mind for the adolescent program from the start. The staff objected at first, saying that she didn't have two years of recovery behind her, but I said, "Let me worry about that." I watched her for about a year, but then I let her go.

* * *

Ridgeview and Talbott provided me with the most sparkling golden opportunity—my own adolescent chemical dependence treatment unit, under Talbott's supervision. It was necessary for us to convert an already existing unit into one that reflected Talbott's philosophy, to hire a new staff, and even to develop and implement an outpatient treatment center and school. This was the second hardest thing I ever had to do, next to getting sober. Many, many days, I felt like Daniel entering the lion's den when I came to work, but ultimately the directors at Ridgeview were supportive. Today this unit enjoys national recognition as a model program.

I officially became director of Ridgeview's adolescent division in 1984 and brought on Harold Smith, an old friend, as my associate director. For the next three years, we guided the program together.

Harold Smith: I went to the U. of A. undergraduate school and medical school. I knew Martha peripherally. I was a drug addict, she was a drug addict. I was into my own stuff and so was she. She preceded me into treatment at Ridgeview by a few months. Basically I'm a junkie, a narcotics addict. I come from a small town in Arkansas called El Dorado, which is about 15 miles from the Louisiana-Arkansas border. My mom was the principal of my elementary school, and my dad was the principal of my high school. At college, I got in the "right" fraternity. We did a lot of drugs, but I was a 4.0 student and I was able to maintain a certain discipline about my education, but my personal life was trashed up.

I never finished college because I managed to get into medical school after my junior year. I got married between my junior year of college and my freshman year of medical school. That marriage lasted about a year. I was twenty by then, but emotionally I was thirteen or fourteen years old. I got married again at the height of my addiction, during my residency in

Tuscaloosa, Alabama; I wanted to be a family practitioner, a country doctor. By the time I got into treatment, I was thirty and had a three-year-old son.

I was committed four times between 1978 and 1982. The fourth time, I was in this hospital down in Louisiana, having tremendous blackouts. They never would detox me, because you only detox drug addicts and they figured that a doctor couldn't possibly be a drug addict.

For almost five years I was in and out of various hospitals. Finally, someone gave me the name of this guy, Doug Talbott, who treated addicted doctors down in Georgia.

So I went to Ridgeview, but my attitude was, just give me the outline of what I have to do to quit having this problem, and I'll be out of your way. The people at Ridgeview were always talking about love and hugging. I'd been alone all my life and I didn't need any of that crap. I blew out of there after four months and went back to Arkansas. I was going through a divorce, I was heavily in debt, I didn't have anything.

I lasted about six weeks after I left Atlanta before I got drunk and suicidal. I called my dad and had him drive me back to Ridgeview. The only person I trusted in the whole world was Martha. So Doug dumped me on her. Martha and I have very similar personalities. In my recovery, she was the first person I decided to trust. When I relapsed and came back, Martha was the only one who was willing to take on my anger. She is not easily intimidated.

Martha and I work well together. We don't have to do a lot of cross-checking. I think she is driven in ways that perhaps some of the rest of us are not. Medicine is a male-dominated profession, and medical school is a very intimidating educational process where women are really put through the ringer. It's tough. To be recognized as an outstanding doctor, a woman has to do just that little bit extra. I also think that because Doug went to bat for her, Martha felt she had to prove that she didn't get ahead because of Doug.

I owe a great deal of my early sobriety to Doug and Martha. Today I am once again a fully functioning physician—free of the bondage of my active addiction. I have remarried and my wife and I continue to grow.

I have always admired Martha's ability to communicate with people. She can extend herself to others so that they feel she is genuinely interested in what they are doing. She is capable of endearing herself in a very respectful way.

What I like about Martha is that she has no hidden motives. What you see is what you get. Her intent is to help people, and that's why it is so refreshing to deal with her. If you're looking for Martha, look straight in front of you—at the headlight of the oncoming train.

Our treatment team at Ridgeview functioned like a family. In the past, I had never been able to play as a team member. I always had to stand alone. Today I'm never alone, at work or at play; I'm always a part of a family.

During these years, Talbott also stood by me through three surgical procedures, one of which was very serious. Once I got sober, I began to pay the price of years of addiction. An old knee injury became an acute problem. Later I had to have surgery on my right thumb. Talbott managed the pain medication required for these procedures, guarding against reactivation of my chemical dependence. He also provided a tremendous amount of emotional support.

The most frightening operation came in May 1985. After I had endured months of excruciating shoulder pain, doctors diagnosed a herniated disk in my neck, and I underwent neck surgery and an anterior cervical discectomy. Talbott, gloved and gowned, watched over me. He had always been there for me, and I, in turn, tried to be there for him, once I got well enough.

My personal life at that time was often as full and frequently more traumatic than my professional life. I'd had the two relationships early on in recovery, so I figured I had worked through my addictive problems with men. Then I met Justin. He was the producer of one of the many TV programs that featured me once I began lecturing. He was quite a lot older than I, sophisticated, charming, urbane. I fell madly, head over heels, addictively in love with him.

For a while, our relationship was a mad whirl. He lived in New York, so I would fly up on weekends and rarely leave his apartment while I was in town. If he was traveling, I would often hop on a plane and join him in Houston or L.A. or wherever he happened to be. It was glamorous and exciting— I'd never known a man like him. But it didn't take long for the addictiveness of the affair to turn sour for both of us. If our relationship was going to develop further, he had to move to Atlanta or I had to move to New York. For various reasons, neither one of us would budge. What's worse, we became jealous of each other's work: I resented the time he spent at the studio, he resented my time at the hospital. My first clue that things were not right came in a series of dreams I had about two months after we met.

In my dream I spent most of the night shooting cocaine and morphine and dealing dope for the money. I shot. I sweat. I shot more. I copped and stayed loaded all night long.

It was incredibly real; I was right back in the center of the action. I experienced all the old feelings, the old behavior patterns, the paranoia, the sense of being inevitably, irresistibly trapped by the dragon of the disease. I thought I was hopelessly entangled in the all-encompassing web of active addiction.

I recorded one of these dreams, and the diary entry sounds as though I had never stopped using:

March 3, 1983
I picked up the syringe and drew up the coke from the spoon, previously burned and blackened from

— 217 —

cooking down the junk: 20 units of pure USP (500 mgs).

I tied myself off—I needed no one and wanted no one. I had everything I needed and wanted and loved in that one syringe and in the plastic bag in my pocket. My veins stood out. They were clean from eighteen months of abstinence.

A rush. I knew what it would feel like. I could get off again. And I had wanted this all along. I popped the point of the needle in. It was just like it used to be. No problem. Registering immediately. The pinprick, the increasing power. The blood appears in the cartridge of the syringe and swirls psychedelically. Clear solution and deep red blood encircle each other. I tap the plunger.

Wham! The hydrochloride taste in the back of my throat. Tachycardia ensues. Vision blurs and the top of my head shoots off in a dynamic burst of rockets, stars, and energetic propulsion. Oh, yes; total body, mind, and soul orgasm. Flash! Here comes that same old feeling again. Flash! Paradise. Flash! Instantaneous burst of power and pleasure. Flash! Total intensity and stimulation. Flash! The world in a syringe. Pure, unadulterated energy and pleasure.

I register again and boot it again, and again, and again. Once is not enough. Never can I get enough. I withdraw the needle and the thick red liquid oozes out rapidly. Pressure must be 220 over 160. Pulse up to 240—a new record.

I stagger to the sink and rinse the syringe. Time is not determinable. There might as well be no such thing. Quickly I drop 2 grains (128 mg) of morphine (no Demerol available tonight and good heroin is practically impossible to come by these days) into the fit and draw up another 20 units of water (shake

*and bake). The saccharinlike tablets dissolve almost
immediately.*

*I tie off and jab the spike in, already beginning to
rush, and fire up the morphine. Wham! About face.
Excruciating pins and needles and the hydrochloride taste is overpowering.*

*A ton of bricks on my chest. Breathing is difficult.
The inevitable arrhythmias ensue. Fear? Why not?
It's all part of the web. I anticipate it. I grab on for
all it's worth. The closer I come, the more intense the
experience, the adventure, the challenge. Time is
nonexistent. The nod (drowsiness), the hallucinations. Truly a roller coaster of the most intense,
instantaneous experiences imaginable.*

*The chemicals jerk you up, down, around, and
inside out at a pace only God can perceive. Excuse
me while I kiss the sky—and nearly die.*

When Justin and I were together, we were ecstatic. When
we were apart, it was hell. I thought I would die if I didn't talk
to him every day. I missed him terribly when we were apart. I
wanted more than anything to call him, to hear his voice—
better yet, to wake up in his arms. I could not seem to let go of
him or let go of what we had.

It took months for me to get over this relationship. We
began to break apart after six months, and it took another four
or five months before I felt sure that I would not use and
would not kill myself.

By December 1983, I felt completely wasted. I had been
sober for more than two years. I had suffered through three
nearly devastating love relationships. But I still buried myself
in my work, and felt lonely and utterly hopeless.

Doc Talbott and his wife, Polly, with whom I'd also become
close, invited me to the Florida Keys for Christmas that year. I
was excited about going, but I was also anxious. I thought

they were just being nice—after all, it was Christmas.

On the night before I left, I wrote a startling entry in my diary. My drug fantasies were no longer confined to dreams; they were daydreams, conscious evocations of the glories of dope.

December 20, 1983

   The relief—to get away from it all. A few more weeks—days maybe—and I really think it could have done me in. The agony of the last three months has been incredible . . . the stress, the gray hairs, the loneliness, the frustration, the desire to tell them all to get screwed, the desire to use, and not necessarily in that order.

   After having been through hell and back a hundred times over, knowing I have a fatal disease, knowing that regardless of the agony and torment facing me at the present—the agony and torment of the past is a thousand times worse. And I still want to use. Four weeks ago, I decided I could drink again. After all, I'm off Antabuse; my tolerance would be back up, and I always handled my liquor so well. How about that for insanity? And it gets better (or worse, whatever the case may be). So then, one day I am looking at my veins in the sauna at the fitness center. I'm really in excellent physical health, and my veins are finally back in great shape. And after all, it's been over two years. I could get off on a few hits of coke. In fact, my veins are so great that I wouldn't even have to tie off—just pop that needle in. Just for one day, a couple of grams or so. Note— not just one hit—I have no delusions regarding that. My thoughts in the sauna: I really don't want to go back and walk in hell, but I've got to have some temporary relief and nothing provides that like coke.

No one would even have to know; just take a couple of days off. Then, last night, when my vacation began, I almost went into the liquor store. A fifth of Southern Comfort to celebrate my survival thus far—and the beginning of vacation. No problem. No one would know.

It's killing me. That's what running my own chemical dependence unit for adolescents—in one of the finest institutes in the country—is doing to me. It's chewing me up and spitting me out. My endorphins are nearly as depleted now as they were when I came into treatment. I really can't stand it. I'm losing it. It's changing me instead of me changing it. I'm not as strong as I thought. And if I quit? No way. I've said I'll do it or die and I'll do just that. And I may die trying.

This is depressing the shit out of me. Where am I going? Why? With whom? I used to know. Don't use, go to meetings, work the steps. It's all there is. Well, screw every last one of you. I don't, I have been, and I do. I pray. I do the best I can with what I've got. I feel as if I've already done the impossible. And you want more, don't you? What happens when I don't have it to give—which is now. I just don't have any more. Not for me, not for you, not for anyone.

God help me. I'm going down fast. It's a lonely and long road.

Well, as God had promised, the sun did shine again in the midst of the storm, and I didn't go down. Instead, I let go again, and what was waiting was beyond dreams.

15
FLORIDA FANTASIES

*The Heart has reasons
which reasons
know nothing of.*
BLAISE PASCAL

On December 21, 1983, I flew in a little thirteen-seat prop plane to Key West to spend Christmas with my "adopted family," the Talbotts, at their Florida home, which they referred to as "Camp Cudjoe, the sanctuary by the sea." I was exhausted and in desperate need of a vacation. In addition to feeling overwhelmed by my work and depressed by my personal life, I harbored some trepidation about spending a week with the Talbotts. Although I'd spent Thanksgiving with them on two previous occasions, I knew Christmas was a special family holiday for them, and they didn't accept outsiders easily.

Fog Talbott: Martha—or Rosie, as she's known in our family—coming to the Keys that year was very symbolic because that was the first time Mom and Dad had included an outsider in our family Christmas. Christmastime has always been a big thing in our family, steeped in tradition and ritual. The fact that they invited Rosie was a statement that they had accepted her into the family.

* * *

As soon as I set foot on Key West soil, smelled the sweet air, and felt the warm breeze on my face, I fell in love with it. Doc and Polly picked me up at the airport, and then we stopped on the 21-mile causeway between Key West and Cudjoe Key to buy fresh-picked oranges at a fruit stand and fresh-caught shrimp at a dock. That afternoon, we sat on the deck of the Talbott house and gazed out over Cudjoe Bay at the American shoals and out into the Atlantic. This "million-dollar view" was breathtaking, and just what I needed to begin to relax.

By 1983, I'd known Doc for more than two years and was already well acquainted with Polly Talbott, who worked at GADA, and with little Polly (Pooh), who was then about nineteen, the youngest of the six Talbott kids. Pooh and I had gotten to be friends months before when she attended an addiction conference in Knoxville, Tennessee, with Doc and me. We shared a room, went to the World's Fair, and drove back to Atlanta together.

In July 1982, I had been invited to Richard Talbott's wedding and had met all the other family members. Richard, whose nickname for some reason is Bob, is the fourth Talbott child. Bob and his wife, Sue, were the only other family members who lived in the Atlanta area. We later became quite close, but at the time of their wedding I didn't know the family well and I felt rather awkward.

It was an absolutely grand affair, held in the Talbotts' beautiful backyard in Atlanta. I met Mark Talbott (Geeks), a professional squash player who is ranked number one in the world; David (Bean), also a professional squash player and a squash coach at Yale; and Wendy, the oldest of the Talbott clan and a Ph.D. psychologist working in the addiction treatment field in Columbus, Ohio. Also present at the wedding was Doug Talbott, Jr.

For months, Polly had been telling me about her bright, handsome bachelor son who was an IBM systems engineer in Baltimore. I later found out that whenever an opportunity arose, she had been mentioning me to him. When Doug and I first met at Bob and Sue's wedding, we were not particularly impressed with each other, and our conversation was brief.

However, Momma knew best, and she refused to give up. On September 12, 1983, after my second sobriety birthday celebration, Polly asked me to join the Talbotts for dinner. Doc and Polly planned to meet Bob and Sue at the Mansion, an elegant Atlanta restaurant, for dinner. Doug, Jr., just happened to be in town for an IBM workshop—and just happened to be seated next to me at dinner. This time, Doug—or Fog, as he is known in the family—and I hit it off very well. Following dinner, the rest of the family disappeared, and Polly instructed me to drop Fog at his hotel, since it was on my way home. Actually, his hotel was no more convenient to me than it was to them, so this appeared to me to be a very interesting maneuver.

G. Douglas Talbott: Polly thought Martha and Fog ought to get together. I said, "You're out of your cotton-picking mind. Those two people are as different as night and day." But Polly just said, "You are so bright in some ways and so dumb in others."

Fog asked me out the following night for dinner and a movie. I, of course, accepted, not particularly wishing to hurt the eldest son and namesake of my boss, friend, and surrogate father, but I was consumed with mixed feelings. Fog was very bright, attractive, and fun, but he wasn't really my type—whatever that was. This situation appeared to me to be potentially explosive, to put it mildly. I valued my friendship with Doc and the relationship I had with Polly, Bob, Sue, and Pooh too much to risk upsetting the balance. Nonetheless, hormones prevailed, but both of us proceeded with discretion and moderation—modes of operating that were rather new to me.

The following night, we went to see *Trading Places,* then stayed up until 3:00 A.M. talking. Something clicked—not with the all-consuming, addictive intensity with which I had begun every other relationship, but slowly. This relationship was more delicate, more restrained. The last thing in the world I wanted—next to a drug relapse—was to be hurt again, and I sensed the same in Fog. We were sensitive to each other's needs and feelings. From the beginning, we were honest and open; we didn't try to control, dominate, or possess each other. Over the next few months we talked frequently over the phone, getting to know each other better and better.

When we then met again that Christmas in Key West with the rest of the family, I was a little uneasy. I wasn't quite sure what would happen. With the Talbotts, nothing is private and certainly nothing is sacred. So in the midst of their nuttiness, our mutual fondness grew to friendship and friendship grew to respect, trust, and love. We fished, we dined, we played squash, we went scuba diving, we talked for endless hours, and we basked in freedom and joy with the family.

Our long-distance relationship intensified after I returned to Atlanta and he to Baltimore, and we began to visit each other frequently. In March 1984, Fog made the decision to move to Atlanta and transfer to IBM's divisional headquarters. In July, we moved together into a condo I had purchased. To celebrate, we set off for the Keys once again on vacation.

Fog Talbott: In many ways, my story is the classic "child of an alcoholic" story. I'm the second-oldest of six kids. My parents were incredibly busy, then incredibly sick, so not surprisingly, I became a typical "caretaker." We have a very competitive successful family, and it's easy to get swallowed up in all the hype and recognition, and to lose one's own sense of identity in the process.

In my other relationships, the women were dependent on me and there wasn't much sharing. My relationships tended to be extensions of the caretaking role I had adopted at home. I chose women who needed to be taken care of, and they, in turn, worshiped me, which was very unhealthy because ultimately those roles break down. With Rosie, I experienced a totally different sort of relationship.

In October 1984, Doc celebrated his sixtieth birthday at a gala affair. All the kids assembled at the Talbott home in Atlanta for a special party plus a weekend of typical Talbott frenetic activity. (Thanks to Bob, I fractured a rib during a Saturday morning football game; however, I was voted All-Pro for my amazing tight-end abilities.) During the weekend, two family friends, J.R. and Blanche, began exerting some heavy pressure regarding formal plans for the next family wedding— mine and Fog's. They insisted it had to be in the Keys, on the deck overlooking Cudjoe Bay. I didn't argue the point.

Fog Talbott: Until I got to know Rosie, it had never entered my mind to think about marrying somebody who had an alcohol and drug problem. I knew that a history of addiction would not totally preclude a relationship, but it would make me very cautious. I was so fed up with being Mr. Florence Nightingale that the last thing I wanted was a relationship where I might end up being a caretaker. But Rosie was different; she was strong enough and far enough into her recovery so that the chances of a relapse were minimized. My parents thought we were the best match they'd seen. They had met the whole litany of women I'd dated. They felt Rosie and I were good together. A lot of marriages set up by parents are disasters; the bias factor can be so destructive.

Ours is a difficult family to be accepted into. The standards are unspoken, but high. It's a very competitive family— aggressive, achievement-oriented and successful. It's also very close and very protective. Being accepted by this family is rather like getting into a very elite club. It's very difficult and very demanding—picky and choosy. The fact that Rosie fit in so quickly and easily was a good sign.

On October 23, 1984, at midnight, Fog proposed to me. I was lying in our water bed watching the *Tonight Show* because Paul McCartney was a guest. Fog came down the stairs yelling, "Turn off the TV." I replied, "Hell, no—don't you realize McCartney is on!" The next thing I knew the TV was off, Fog was carrying a gorgeous bouquet of red roses and a chocolate cake with red roses all over it—to symbolize my new nickname, Rosie. He handed me a letter with the heading: "A chocolate and Rosie proposal." (I am also a chocoholic.) The letter read:

> *Of all the loves I have known,*
> *I loudly proclaim from Atlanta to Rome*
> *That none share our love better than we.*
> *My darling Rosie, will you marry me?*

Rarely caught unprepared, I just happened to have my own little card in the bedside dresser, which I immediately brought forth. It read:

> *Roses are yellow;*
> *The sky is blue.*
> *You're my fellow,*
> *The answer is . . . I do!*

Fog Talbott: I proposed to Rosie on October 23, 1984. So here it was after midnight—and we felt we had to call somebody. Dad was in Chicago on some trip, but we really wanted to tell him. Of course, waking Dad up in the middle of the night is a gas. He goes to sleep about ten and gets totally freaked if you wake him up. He was really excited by the good news, though. This was what he and Mom had been praying for. Apparently, after he talked to us, he was so disoriented that he got up, got dressed, and went down to the coffee shop to get breakfast, but the coffee shop wasn't open because it was only two in the morning.

He sent us a telegram that said, "To the two people I love the most in the world. I'm so happy for you. Couldn't sleep a wink last night. Please send Dalmane."

My feelings for Fog were dramatically different from those I'd had for other men in my life, and I really knew that this was right and good. I realized that Fog had not been put in my life until I was ready for this relationship—so I would cherish him, not possess him; trust him, not demand from him; be open with him, not control him; be honest with him, not live with secrets and lies; be willing to share with him, not dominate him; and love him, not depend on him.

Our wedding announcement was slightly unorthodox, but we felt it suited us:

Mr. & Mrs. D. E. Morrison & Dr. & Mrs. G. D. Talbott

Proudly announce the Engagement

& Forthcoming Nuptial Ceremony

of their daughter & son

Rosie & Fog

Much to the Joyous Relief of

Both Families, the Church & the IRS

Cudjoe Key, Florida

12–24–84

Fog Talbott: The guy who married us, Bob, is a good friend—an ex–Episcopal priest who is now a real-estate agent in the Keys. Every year he has a neat Christmas party and midnight mass in his incredibly beautiful house right on the ocean. I called Bob and asked him to marry us. He said he'd love to, but he thought it might be a problem to marry us as a priest because Rosie had been married before. However, he was able to marry us in his capacity as a justice of the peace. Nevertheless, he wore his vestments and read from the Bible and the Book of Common Prayer. It was a traditional ceremony in that sense.

It was perfect because we just had family and a few very close friends. It was a very special day.

On December 21, 1984, we flew into Key West just in time to make it to the Monroe County Courthouse to obtain our marriage license.

Momma (Polly) formed an organization she called WHAT, Wedding Headquarters Assigned Tasks, and designated herself Grandmaster Extraplenipotentiary—ultimate central commander of the events.

Our pre-wedding party was held at our favorite restaurant, Coco's Cantina, a local Cuban dive about a quarter-mile from the house. The lighted sign out front read:

COCO'S CANTINA

I DID

I DO

I WILL

ROSIE AND FOG

A very colorful Key West band, the Survivors, played at the party while we danced, ate yellowtail snapper with black beans and rice, and drank Cuban coffee. The main event of the evening proved to be the skit. Doc, Bean, Geeks, Bob, Sue, Pooh, Wendy, Blanche, and J.R. performed short takeoffs on some of Fog's more significant previous relationships with women. It was obscene, totally indiscreet, and an absolute riot. The Morals Committee (J.R. and Philip) were not able to maintain any semblance of control. For the finale, J.R. rushed in dressed as Cupid in black bikini underwear, with a halo, black wings and mask, and a bow and arrow. He shot an arrow at Fog and me, then charged up onto the bar and nearly lost his head in the blades of a ceiling fan. Fog and I howled with laughter.

Following the party at Coco's, we discovered the night was not yet over. After we returned to the house, the men suddenly attacked Fog, tied him up, blindfolded him, and carried him off. I thought I'd lost him forever amid all this insanity when I was suddenly accosted in a similar manner by the women. Blindfolded and loosely bound, I was led to a power boat, and we headed out onto the canal. Soon I could hear the guys' voices; they were obviously anchored nearby in the other power boat. I was ordered to get into the boat with Fog. Then the others took off in the second boat, leaving us without a key to our boat. It was an absolute riot. Needless to say, we did not remain bound for the rest of the night, but we did remain anchored in the channel at sea. It was one of the most wondrous nights of my life.

We returned to the house at nine o'clock the next morning, cleaned up, and got ready for the wedding, which was to be at noon. The entire deck was decorated with orchids intertwined through the railings. I wore a simple white cotton dress and carried a gorgeous bouquet of red hibiscus. Polly gave me an engraved gold bracelet that had been her great aunt's. Pooh lent me her gold chain bracelet, and Blanche gave me a new blue garter. I was ready: old, new, borrowed, and blue.

I was very nervous when I heard the music begin (a tape, administered by J.R.) and saw Doc waiting at the foot of the stairs to escort me to Fog and then serve as Fog's best man. Momma was my matron of honor. My nervousness left me after a few moments, and this became the happiest and most joyful celebration I had ever known. It was a totally fantastic experience—as spiritual as anything I've ever known. The sun and sea only served to accentuate the beauty and goodness of my family, my friends, the ceremony, and the love that was so evident. Surely this was the essence of joy, happiness, and a new freedom.

Fog and I honeymooned in the Keys, fishing, playing squash, scuba diving, and enjoying each other. The Keys are very special to us as a family and as a couple.

Fog Talbott: If you were to describe our relationship in one word, it would be "sharing." We don't play the traditional roles in our marriage. In essence, it's sort of a role reversal—I could be a very good house husband, I suppose; I've even offered to do that. Our marriage is a nice balance between dependency and independence. We're both very involved in our own careers and our own interests, yet we are able to share. We play squash together a lot, we go to the club together a lot, we're film addicts, we share interests, like reading, scuba diving, fishing, shooting, going to concerts— yet there's nothing compulsive about our activities. There's none of that unhealthy co-dependency that you see in a lot of couples, where one partner inhales and the other exhales.

Our priorities are clearly established. For me, Rosie is first, my family is second, my friends are third, work is fourth. I'm not saying it's the same for Rosie, but I am saying that work isn't everything to us. That's where the balancing and sharing come in. We try new things; we like to travel. We're good friends. I've never had that kind of relationship before.

Fog and I are truly happy together; our marriage is, quite honestly, indescribable. For the first time, I am involved in a relationship that began innocently, grew steadily, and blossomed into a wonderful togetherness based on sharing with and caring about each other. I realize that God did for me what I was not able to do for myself. And I am so very grateful.

16
ONE DAY AT A TIME

For yesterday is but a dream
And tomorrow is only a vision
But today well lived
Makes every yesterday a dream of happiness
And every tomorrow a vision of hope.
Look well, therefore, to this day.

SANSKRIT PROVERB

It was a step of utmost honesty for me to admit that I had a disease called addiction and that I was powerless over it. I know what it is like to walk in darkness. I know the torment, agony, desperation, and sense of impending doom one feels when in the grip of addiction. By accepting my total lack of control over my addiction, I also came to understand and to concede that I had to stop trying to dominate other people and situations. Then, and only then, did I begin to grow.

After I had hurt badly enough and long enough, I came to believe that only God could help me. Paradoxically, once I "surrendered," I found hope. I stopped feeling that I had to rely solely on myself and began to have true faith in a Power outside myself. Nietzsche once said: "That which does not kill us makes us stronger." There is little doubt in my mind that this is true because I had to nearly die before I found the God of my understanding and therein found real strength.

My purpose in life is to carry this message: Addiction is a treatable disease; there is health, hope, and freedom through recovery. That, I hope, is what this book is about. I keep what I have by giving it away, and it is my hope that by sharing my experiences, I will help someone else. Carrying the message is a service; I am simply a servant.

I believe recovery is an ongoing daily process that brings progress, not perfection. All I ever wanted was to love, to be free, to help others, and to get closer to God. Today I love, I am free, I help others, and I keep trying to get closer to God. All I was looking for was a little peace of mind, but I never knew how to be still and know I was with God. I was trapped in my addiction. Recovery has helped me realize that God does for me what I could not, and still cannot, do for myself. All I have to do is cope with today, this particular twenty-four hour period. I know I can do this with God's help as long as I don't use drugs. He has granted me serenity and peace of mind. What a blessing. More times than not, this simple prayer helps me on a daily basis:

Serenity Prayer

God grant me the Serenity
to accept the things
I cannot change;

Courage to change the
things I can; and

Wisdom to know the
difference.
REINHOLD NEIBUHR

By 1984, I was a full partner in GADA, working with people who supported me, confronted me, listened to me, told me what to do, and let me tell them what to do. Philip Wilson, Arthur Carpenter, Charlie Brown, Jim Blevins, and Harold

Smith were instrumental in my continuing journey in recovery. Philip, in particular, became like a brother to me, and still is.

G. Douglas Talbott: In a treatment facility, it's important to have people who are recovering and also to have people who are not recovering, like Philip. As a recovering alcoholic, I can't see certain things. One of the prices you pay for recovery is that you have some emotional and psychological blinders. But blinders work the other way, too. Sometimes we'll be talking about a patient, and Philip will say, "Why can't you see that?" Then, two minutes later, I'll turn around to Phil and say, "Why can't you see that?"

In the fall of 1985, Philip and I became co-owners of GADA, under Doc's continual supervision. Today we operate a very successful private medical office and several chemical dependence treatment programs, and Philip continues to guide me in these ventures.

I continue to lecture, travel, direct the adolescent chemical dependence program and administer affairs at GADA. I speak frequently about addiction to the American Bar Association, the Atlanta Falcons, the University of Georgia Bulldogs, the Governor's Advisory Council, local chambers of commerce, and numerous school, parent, and adolescent groups. I've continued to participate in national conferences, and several times I have been a guest speaker at the Betty Ford Center in Palm Springs, which I consider a particular honor. Recently I began to work with the Georgia Task Force and AID Atlanta to increase the public's awareness and knowledge of AIDS. I was also particularly fortunate to have participated in a number of women's seminars. In May 1986, I was allowed to implement and open an outpatient treatment program and school for adolescents at Ridgeview called ACTION.

I was sober for five years before I felt that I could come back to Arkansas and stay clean. I had hurt many people—my ex-husbands, my parents and brother, many friends, many colleagues. Even as I worked on this book and relived the events of my past, I felt the sharp stabs of remorse many times.

But an important part of recovery is making peace with the past and going forward. I missed my friends, my parents, and the part of the country where I'd grown up, particularly the lakes and the fine fishing. In 1986, Fog and I bought a house on a bluff overlooking Beaver Lake in Rogers, Arkansas, about 25 miles north of Fayetteville. Now we have the best of both worlds—the terrific oceanfront Talbott home in the Keys and the tranquillity of the lush Ozark countryside in Arkansas. We go up several times a year to visit my parents and friends and do a little fishing. It took a long time before I felt comfortable at home, but today I belong, today I can go home again. This has been another tremendous blessing.

One facet of my life that both bemused and pleased me—an aspect that I realized even early in my recovery—was that despite my addiction, I had managed to maintain the loyalty and love of my friends. I felt intense gratitude again and again as I worked on this book and realized this gift I'd been given.

Maggie Peters: I don't know—is Martha different now? She's gained weight. She has fingernails. She got her teeth fixed. That was our joke. If she went to Atlanta, she was going to let her nails grow and get her teeth fixed.

She's still just as aggressive as can be. Probably more so now. I have always told her that she was so manipulative and grandiose that if she'd been born with facial defects, she'd weasel her way onto the cover of *Vogue* magazine. She still loves to spend money like she always did, so that's nothing new. Her life's still as fast as it always was.

Our friendship has changed. During the first couple of years we knew each other, we were very close, and I don't mean to sound gushy, but when she left, I lost a very good friend. I was very ambivalent about her going to Atlanta because I knew that if she was going to live, I was going to have to lose her as a friend. Which is true. I have given her up to Atlanta; I have given her up to recovery.

Since I've been sober, my relationship with Maggie has definitely changed. I believe she became very co-dependent during that last year before I went into treatment. We haven't been as close since I've been sober. Part of me keeps my distance, I suppose, because I'm afraid I'll get sick again, even without drugs—just in behavior. Maggie has some different perceptions with regard to my illness—lots of discrepancies and varying opinions about herself and about me.

Connie Williams Kingston: Martha hasn't really changed that much. She's changed her life-style; but there's still a lot of care in there. Martha is Martha, which is good.

Martha's and my relationship has changed. When you live with someone, there's a certain kind of closeness, but I feel a certain distance now because we don't have a day-to-day relationship. I can rely on her now, though, in ways I couldn't before. I feel like I got my friend back.

When Martha went into treatment, I started going to Al-Anon. I liked what they had to say, but I didn't stick with it because I couldn't cure my brother or a number of other people I loved. But recently I've gotten involved in another twelve-step program, and I'm coming to realize that change starts with me.

When I went into treatment, several of the therapists and many of the patients commented on the fact that I still had friends. For someone who had taken the amount of dope I'd taken and done the things I'd done, it was remarkable that there was still anybody in my life who cared. Usually addicts alienate everybody. I certainly did—but somehow they still cared about me, particularly Maggie, Connie, my parents, my brother, and even Paul.

Ed Morrison: Martha hasn't changed much. She's still strong-willed, impatient, direct, and outspoken. The biggest change, of course, is that she's clean.

Doyle Morrison: Martha has changed. She's much more congenial, much more concerned about us. She checks with us every week—or even twice a week. She is interested in what we're doing and where we've been. She's very considerate. It even seems to be good between her and her mother.

Eliene Morrison: Martha has changed in some ways, I suppose, but I think the changes have to do with her being off drugs. She's back on an even keel, and she's funnier now—she's more fun to be with. But she's still the Marty I knew when she was a little girl. She always had compassion for everybody—she always had that. Even when she ran away as a teenager, she called us every day and said, "Don't worry about me." Of course, that didn't stop us from worrying, but somehow it made it easier for us. I'd say again—she has compassion for all of us, and that's nothing new.

I believe that God works in strange ways. One of the most startling examples of this came to me as I was working on this book. For more than five years, I'd had no idea who had sent Ron Brooks and Harvey Irwin to save me. I suspected many people—Paul, Connie, the doctors I worked with in Little Rock. It was during my interview with Brad Williams that the truth emerged. The fact that Brad was the messenger seemed like a blessing to me. It was so perfectly right. Brad, too, is now sober and doing well. He has moved out West, has happily remarried, and is at work on his doctorate.

* * *

Brad Williams: My last time in treatment was no different from any other time. I was no sicker than I'd been in the past. I was just lying there, shaking it off for a couple of days, and I thought if I had to depend on myself to make it in life, I might as well give up right now because I couldn't do it. That was my surrender, with a little bit of a spiritual awakening, I guess. It was nothing dramatic. I can't really describe the feeling; all I can do is look back and see that when I came out of treatment that time, I was willing to do some things differently.

I started going to AA meetings. For a while, I just lived from meeting to meeting. I got a sponsor and did what he told me. I changed sponsors several times—one guy was even sicker than I was—but I kept looking. I made friends with the woman who is now my wife, and she introduced me to my present sponsor. I started working the steps, and things started getting better.

In the past, I'd gone to AA for a few months here and there, but I never worked with a sponsor or worked the steps. I would just hang around long enough to dry out and go back to work, but that was as far as it would progress. I didn't grow much. This time, it worked and I feel that I'm growing.

I told Ron Brooks about Martha during a short lucid period in my life. Most times in the past if Connie had come to me wailing about Martha, I would have said, "Tough shit, let the bitch work it out for herself." I think I'm basically a pretty good guy, but when I was drinking those decent parts of me were pretty well hidden a lot of the time.

Ron Brooks: Interventions are a labor of love for me. Now we do them with the help of family, clergy, friends, co-workers—whoever is relevant. In a loving manner, we try to break through to the alcoholic or addict. I try to get people early in the morning when they are coming down and miserable with a hangover or whatever. Then they're not quite so well defended. We tell them that we'll love them until they are ready to love themselves. It's a neat experience to turn somebody's life around.

And life goes on.

One of the greatest changes in my life happened recently when Doc, Philip, the GADA staff, and I decided to leave Ridgeview Institute and start our own treatment programs—Talbott Recovery System. This effort has been challenging and exciting. Our programs provide comprehensive inpatient, outpatient, and family treatment for adults, health professionals, adolescents, and families. We are now associated with another wonderful institution, Anchor Hospital of Atlanta. For me, being on the cutting edge in the field of addictionology with such fine professionals is simply another spiritual opportunity.

My personal life is equally full, with trips to Arkansas and the Keys, and sharing various interests with Fog. I still set challenges for myself whenever possible, and in 1987 I began to prepare for one of my bigger ones.

I had decided to enter—full tilt, as usual—the biggest fishing tournament in North America, the annual Key West Marlin Tournament. This was to be my first fishing tournament, and I hoped to hook my first big marlin. I knew with absolute certainty I would win. Overconfident, I guess, but I researched, worked out "religiously" for six months, and put in my time fishing. In other words, I did the legwork necessary to make it happen. It's my belief that if you do your homework and say a few prayers, good things will happen. And good things did.

On October 21, 1987, my brother, my nephew, and I were the anglers aboard Captain Jim Sharpe's *Sea Boots*. I hooked the Big One. One hour and seven minutes later, we boated a spectacular 11-foot 10-inch 520-pound blue marlin. I had won the tournament, set a new tournament record, and caught the third-largest fish ever caught in the Florida Keys. Another great thrill.

— 239 —

Good things happen when you live life sober. It's not that life sober holds no pain, no disappointment, no conflict. It's just that living sober makes you and everyone else and everything else okay. When you've walked in hell, simply to be okay is a blessing from God. And today I believe God walks with me.

For that part of my past where others were hurt, I'm deeply sorry. For that part of my past where God's grace has been made evident, I'm deeply thankful. For the tomorrows, I'm grateful for the knowledge and support of a God of my understanding. And for the present, one day at a time, I'm eternally grateful for my life and the gift of sobriety.